The Sacraments

Seven Stories of Growth

Joseph Martos, Ph.D.

D1512314

LIGUORI
PUBLICATIONS

One Liguori Drive
Liguori, Missouri 63057-9999
(314) 464-2500

Imprimi Potest:
William A. Nugent, C.SS.R.
Provincial, St. Louis Province
The Redemptorists

Imprimatur:
Monsignor Maurice F. Byrne
Vice Chancellor, Archdiocese of St. Louis

ISBN 0-89243-315-9
Library of Congress Catalog Card Number: 89-063183

Copyright © 1989, Liguori Publications
Printed in U.S.A.

Contents

Foreword

Everybody loves a story. Preachers know that a story can hold people's attention better than the most important, but abstract, ideas.

Sacramental theology is necessarily abstract, or is it? I wondered. What if the most important ideas about the sacraments could be put into stories? Would not that be helpful for people trained in theology?

I decided to try my hand at it. As you read these stories, you will discover that each of the seven stories contains common elements. The most important is the story, which is designed to convey just one or more basic ideas about each of the sacraments.

Another element is preparation for the sacraments. A natural way to weave in questions about the sacraments was to have people ask them during sacrament preparation programs. Such programs are an essential aspect of Catholic parish life and so, when possible, I built the story about people who were preparing for a sacramental celebration. I apologize ahead of time if you do not find your favorite questions answered.

Programs, however, are for people, and so a third important element is the people in these stories. People come in all sizes, shapes, and colors — adults and children, parents and relatives, priests and Sisters, deacons and religious educators, Catholics and non-Catholics. I hope that you will find characters in every story who will speak to you.

The stories are written for people who want to learn more about the sacraments as they are understood in the Catholic Church today. You may pick up this book out of curiosity, or you may be a teacher: in an adult-education program, a high-school class, or in a catechetical class as the RCIA, for example. I hope these stories will make your teaching ministry more enjoyable and more effective. Part of the credit for these stories' effectiveness goes to countless theologians, liturgists, and religious educators who have been engaged in renewal of the sacraments since the Second Vatican Council.

I must also give great credit to Julie Kelemen and to her skill as an editor. As a theology professor, I wanted stories to be informative, but her sense of the art of storytelling added human interest to them.

Joseph Martos

Shifting Gears

(Baptism)

For the first time in his life, George Mays was sitting in a Catholic rectory. He could scarcely believe it. A few years ago, if a fortuneteller had told him he'd be here today, he would have asked for his money back.

This was St. Anne's, not far from the shopping strip where he worked as assistant manager in a Western Auto store. He'd met Father Mike before, but this was the first time he'd met the other people in the room.

This was what might once have been called a parlor with comfortable sofas and chairs for everyone, but the TV in the corner suggested that it also served as a den for the priests. On the walls he noticed mostly religious pictures. One showed a round, smiling pope whom he didn't recognize. There was a drawing of Jesus laughing. George thought that was pretty cool; it made Jesus look like a regular guy you could really talk to. Then, over the sofa were some pictures of people he didn't recognize. The only thing they had in common were the halos around their heads. The tiered curtains and shag carpet gave the room a homey feeling. The candles and the open Bible on the coffee table reminded him of why all of them were there.

As the others introduced themselves, George heard each one tell how they had also come to want to learn more about the Catholic Church.

A man named Phil was not a Catholic, but his wife Margaret was. For years he'd seen her go to Mass every Sunday by herself with the kids, but three years ago he had decided to tag along. Finally he made up his mind to find out more about his wife's religion.

Lucy and Ralph had both been baptized and raised as Catholics, but in the sixties they'd gotten mad at their parish priest and stopped going to church. When they moved into this neighborhood, the couple across the street told them to try St. Anne's — that it might be really different from the church they'd left behind. So they thought they'd come and see for themselves.

Frank and Henrietta were also baptized Catholics, but Henrietta had been divorced before marrying Frank in a civil ceremony. She had thought they could not be Catholics anymore, but a friend suggested that maybe they could find a way to rejoin the Church.

Kathy, Michelle, and Arlene were of varying ages and from different backgrounds, but all had recently decided they might like to join the Catholic Church. They enjoyed comparing notes about what had led them to this meeting. One thing they all seemed to have in common was that they felt something was missing in their lives.

George hoped Michelle would stick around; she was kind of cute.

Now it was George's turn. He cleared his throat and said, "My parents weren't very religious, so I've never been to church much, 'cept with girlfriends."

He went on to explain how his one great love was cars, and by buying, fixing up, and reselling them he had always had enough cash to be independent of his folks.

"I had a rocky time in college," he continued, "and I even got into drugs for a while. My grades got so low that I got expelled from school. I traveled around the country for a while doing odd jobs here and there, having a good time, and trying to stay out of trouble. After feeling sorry for myself for about a year, I decided to get back on the straight and narrow. Well, almost. I got a job as assistant manager at this Western Auto store, but lately my free time seems kind of empty…."

He enjoyed going out with friends for a beer after work, and he enjoyed having a good time with the guys on weekends. George glanced around at everyone listening intently to his story. He thought they all looked so strait-laced, and here he was in jeans and a flannel shirt.

"But a few months ago," said George, "I asked myself, 'Is this all there is to life?' It wasn't long afterward that I met Father Mike in the store. Mike didn't look like a priest when he came there on his day off, and I felt sorry for him with the alternator problems he was having in that boat of an Oldsmobile of his."

George turned to Father Mike and said, chuckling, "Are you ever going to get rid of that old gas hog?"

"I'm very attached to it," Mike said with a sad smile, "It was my father's."

"Well," George said, "Mike seemed to know more about cars than you'd expect a preacher to. We got to talking whenever he came by, and we even went out for a few beers after work." George thought to himself that it must be nice to have something to live for. "So when Mike invited me to come to this meeting at his place, I figured what the hell...why not?" Immediately he wondered if he should have said "heck," but everyone laughed so he figured it was OK.

Father Mike looked different in his Roman collar as he spoke. "There are lots of reasons why people come to these inquiry meetings," Father Mike said, "and many people find the answers to their questions about God and religion and life in the Catholic faith."

He asked the group to come up with some of the questions they would like to have answered about the Church or what Catholics believe about this and that, and they spent the rest of the evening talking about the things that were on their minds.

Just before closing Father Mike introduced Sister Janet, a woman who had been listening and taking notes on what the others had been saying.

"Next week," said Father Mike, "Sister Janet will begin addressing the concerns you've raised. She's the director of this parish program, and she's very good. You've done it for what, four years now?"

The woman smiled and nodded.

"She'll be your leader from now on," said Father Mike, "although I'll be dropping in as a guest from time to time."

George was a little disappointed that he would not be seeing Father Mike at these meetings every week. But he figured he'd come anyway and try it for at least another week because he wanted to hear the answers to his questions and to some of the others that had been raised. Besides, he'd still be able to see Father Mike when he came in to buy things for the Olds.

❋ ❋ ❋

George made it to all but one of the meetings during the next four weeks. That was the night he had gone to a birthday party at his sister's house. "It's strange," he had thought to himself as he watched his nephew blow out the candles, "but the way I feel with my sister's family is a little like the way I've been feeling at our meetings in the rectory."

At the last meeting Sister Janet had said, "You all came here a month ago to find out more about the Catholic Church and the way we understand and try to live the Christian life. Since then you've not only been hearing the answers to your questions, but you've also been experiencing them. You've begun to taste what it's like to be a member of the Catholic family. So now the time has come for you to ask yourself if you really want to take the first step toward becoming a Catholic."

George was not completely ready for this step. "Can we change our minds later, if we want to?"

"Nobody will force you. God's gifts are free. If you feel it isn't right for you, you can withdraw from the program anytime."

Michelle was one of the people in the group who admitted that she wouldn't feel right about going on with the group right now. "My answers about the Catholic faith have been answered," she said, "and I really like you all. But I have so many questions about other religions too. To be honest, I think I'd rather do some more looking before I make up my mind." Michelle asked if she could stay until the end of the meeting, though, since she'd like to learn a little about what was coming up for the others. Of course, no one objected, although George was a little sad. Michelle had asked some tough questions and she seemed really smart too, not just cute.

Sister Janet explained that they would be entering the RCIA program beginning next week. "RCIA stands for Rite of Christian Initiation of Adults," she said, "People who are born into Catholic families are generally baptized as infants, but the Church recognizes that being a Christian is an adult responsibility. Even children who are baptized before they can make their own decisions get confirmed when they are older. And, of course, at the beginning of Christian history it was mainly adults who were baptized when they declared their belief in Christ as their Savior. For this reason Christian initiation in the Catholic Church is a program that helps adults go from initial interest to full membership in the Church."

"It sounds like it might take a long time," said Phil. "I've been married to a Catholic for nine years now, but it seems that Margaret is always coming up with things I've never heard of before!"

"You don't have to know *everything* about the Church to be a Catholic," answered Sister Janet. "If that was the requirement, I probably wouldn't be a Catholic yet myself! You just have to know the basics. But what's more important is that you have time to think about and decide for yourself if you want to practice the Christian life the way a Catholic does. That's the main reason behind the RCIA process.

"One of the phrases you'll be hearing a lot the next few months is *new life*. Becoming a Christian means entering a new life, a life with new beliefs, new values, new commitments, and a new relationship with God and the Church. In the early centuries of Christianity, when most people grew up in a pagan world that didn't know about Christ, the initiation process sometimes took as long as three years. The modern RCIA program, however, usually takes about six months."

"So we'll be done in the spring?" asked Phil.

"Yes, you'll be baptized and confirmed near Easter time, if you stay in the program until its end."

"But what about those of us who have already been baptized and confirmed?" inquired Lucy.

"The RCIA program in the United States is not just for unbaptized persons. Technically, the program was designed for new converts to Christianity, and it is used that way in many parts of the world. The way we do it here, however, it's also for people like you and Ralph...and Frank and Henrietta, I might add. Technically, you don't *have* to join the program if you don't want to. You could just go to the pastor and talk over your separation from the Church with him. Then you could be received back into full membership in the Church through the sacrament of Reconciliation. But since *Baptism* means 'immersion,' a lot of people find that the RCIA is an ideal way of gradually wading back into the Church, so to speak, instead of just jumping back into it with both feet. They learn a lot about the Church, and about themselves, in the process."

"But you didn't say anything about whether those of us who are already Catholic will be baptized again," said Lucy.

"Oh, yes. You may recall from having seen other baptisms that during the ceremony people are asked to affirm their faith in God, and they promise to live up to their faith in the Church. When you were baptized as a baby, your parents made those promises for you. This Easter you'll be asked to renew your baptismal promises for yourself as an adult. But you won't be baptized the way the others will."

"I was baptized in the Lutheran Church," said Kathy. "Will I be baptized again?"

"Catholics recognize Baptism in any church as Baptism into the life of Christ, even if it's lived with those outside the Catholic Church. That's the way it has been with us ever since the earliest days of our history. Even though there were no Protestant denominations then, there were still heretical groups who were separated one way or another from the universal Church. When they were received back into the Church, they were not rebaptized, and so you won't have to be either. Like the others who were baptized into the Christian faith once before, you'll only have to renew your baptismal promises."

"So when does the indoctrination begin?" asked Phil with a smile.

His wife looked at him and said, "You make it sound so *medieval,* Phil!"

"Let's think of it more as instruction," said Sister Janet. "Officially, those of you who go on in the program will be known as *catechumens,* and this period of instruction will be your *catechumenate.* Those are words that have a long history in the Church, coming from a Greek word meaning 'one who is being taught orally.' The instruction that you will receive is known as *catechesis,* or preparation for Baptism."

"Well, when do we start?" asked Phil again.

"Before we can begin, you will participate in a ceremony to enroll you in the order of catechumens. That will be a week from Saturday. At next week's meeting, I'll go over that ceremony with you, so you'll know what to do. Does everyone except Michelle want to come for that next time?"

Everyone nodded.

"Arlene and George," invited Janet, "you've both been rather quiet tonight. Do you want to take this first step toward becoming members of the Church?"

"Yes," said Arlene.

George looked around and said, "Uh-huh."

"Wonderful. That leaves only one last thing to do before we close for the evening. Those of you who are familiar with Catholic Baptism may remember sponsors or godparents."

"That was my Uncle Joe and Aunt Mary," said Frank.

"Are they still living, and living nearby?" asked Sister Janet.

"Sure."

"Then you may want to ask them to be your sponsors again, as you rejoin the Church. How do you think they'd feel about that?"

"I think they'd feel the lost sheep had finally got hooked and dragged back into the flock!" said Frank.

"Well, if you'd like to ask them to be your sponsors, you can do that. Or you could ask someone else here in St. Anne's Parish. It should be someone who's active in the Church and preferably someone you can talk over your decision with during the months to come. For most of you, it will probably be the person who got you interested in joining or rejoining the Church."

"Why do you need a sponsor anyway?" inquired George.

"In the earliest days of the Church, there were not many Christians around, and so the community wanted to make sure that each new candidate for Baptism had at least one person who would vouch for their character and their sincerity. It was like having a big brother or big sister in the Church. Since they helped the candidate to be born into the life of God, they eventually came to be called *godparents*. After your Baptism your sponsor will become your godparent."

"Can priests be godparents, even though they're not married?" asked George.

Sister Janet smiled. "I'm sure Father Mike would be very pleased if you asked him to be your sponsor."

❄ ❄ ❄

At the next week's meeting, Father Mike walked with the group over to the church building to explain the first step: Acceptance Into the Order of Catechumens. He pointed out where everyone would sit and assured George that because the pastor, Father Henry, would be presiding at the ceremony, it would be easy for George and him to sit together just like all the other candidates and sponsors. George breathed his own little sigh of relief, because having his friend

13

nearby would help him feel more comfortable in the strange sur-roundings. As it turned out, though, George began to feel more at home around the parish even when Mike was not there.

A week later as the group gathered for the special rite, George looked around and realized that he already knew a number of the people who had gathered in front of St. Anne's. Through them he was meeting others, such as the families and friends of his RCIA group.

Many of the new faces were also connected in one way or another with the RCIA program. John, the deacon who would be joining them for some of their meetings, came up and said hello. Frances, the parish religious education director, mentioned how she had been locating instructors for some of the talks they would be hearing. Some of the others were from the liturgy committee or hospitality ministry who had prepared the ceremony or the reception that would follow. The rest were people who had been in his shoes at one time and were now attending because they had gotten special invitations to come and lend support to the new candidates.

Everyone was glad for the good weather, since Father Henry liked to perform the first part of this ceremony just outside the front doors. Then he would go inside for the second part, to symbolize the entrance of the candidates into the Church. Once they became catechumens, they would already be members of the Church to some extent. Some of the early Christian martyrs, Sister Janet had told them, died before they had been officially baptized, but they were still regarded as Catholic saints.

When Father Henry appeared in the doorway, George and the other candidates stood side by side in front of him, while their sponsors stood directly behind them. After the pastor said a few words of greeting and a prayer, Sister Janet introduced the can-didates to him. He spoke briefly about what it means to be a Christian and a Catholic, after which he asked the candidates what they were asking of the Church.

One by one they each said in their own words why they were there. George said, "I want to learn more about the Catholic faith," but inwardly he wanted to *belong* somewhere, and he wanted to find a better sense of purpose in his life.

Father Henry made a sign of the cross with his thumb on their foreheads, after which they turned around to face the group behind them. Then their sponsors also signed them with the cross. Father Mike had not said anything about applause at this point, but someone in the crowd started clapping, and everyone joined in while George and the other candidates smiled a little self-consciously.

Turning around again, the candidates joined the pastor as he proceeded into the church, led by Deacon John who elevated a large, leather-bound Bible high enough for all to see. The candidates filed into the first pew and the sponsors into the one behind them. Everyone stood while the deacon read the Gospel story about Jesus feeding the multitude with just a few loaves and fish.

Father Henry gave a brief sermon, or homily, as George was learning to call it, explaining the Scripture reading and showing how its lesson could be applied to the lives of all Christians, catechumens and regular Catholics alike. The sermon was a lot shorter than the ones he had usually heard in other churches. George liked that.

The sermon even ended with a surprise as Father Henry wrapped it up, saying, "The Word of God is important for everyone who wants to live according to the Gospel, and so tonight I want to present you with a very readable translation of the New Testament. You may already have a Bible of your own, but I'd like you to accept this one as my way of saying welcome to our family. This book contains the Good News of what we're all about, and I'd like you to read it during the coming months before you make your final decision about joining or rejoining the Catholic Church."

After Deacon John gave each of them their gift-wrapped New Testaments, Father Henry continued: "You should have a good understanding of the new life that Jesus made possible for us before you decide whether you really want to get into it fully by being baptized. For right now, though, we're glad you're here."

This time it was Father Henry who started the applause. Again, George felt both pleased and embarrassed about all the fuss.

"At this point, the instructions in the RCIA say that the candidates should remain together for a while 'to share their fraternal joy and spiritual experiences.' Tonight's reading was on Jesus feeding a large crowd, and here at St. Anne's we like to give the newcomers a real feeling for what that Bible passage is about. We go in for what is technically known as 'experiential catechesis.' For those of you who don't know the lingo yet, it means you're all invited to a covered-dish supper prepared by the good folks in our hospitality ministry!"

As they walked over to the parish center, Father Mike put his hand on George's shoulder and asked, "Well, how does it feel to be a catechumen?"

Mike smiled, saying, "A few weeks ago I couldn't even pronounce the word, and today I'm one of them!"

✸   ✸   ✸

Over the fall and winter months George often reminded himself that he was indeed a "learner." He was learning a lot, not only from the talks at the group meetings but also from listening to parishioners. Father Henry, it was obvious, heavily emphasized the Scriptures, and part of every weekly meeting was spent listening to ordinary Catholics explain what a Scripture passage meant to them.

The sponsors and catechists described how they tried to live the Word of God as parents and singles, at home, on the job, and in volunteer work.

Fred, an electrician, said, "I take Jesus' teaching about 'walking the extra mile' to mean that when you do a job you should double-check to see that it's done well and safely, even if it means working later than you planned on."

Roberta said she remembered the story of Jesus and the woman caught in adultery when her own children got caught doing something that they shouldn't: "It can be really hard to show compassion like Jesus did in those kinds of situations."

Andy recalled one of his favorite Scripture verses, "I often think about the one where Paul said 'I have become all things to all, to save at least some.' It inspires me as a high school teacher and catechist to always try to meet people where they are."

Sister Janet said that when she was younger she had tried to live according to the Word of God for a very simple reason — to get into heaven. "But then I came across the place where Jesus says that those who follow his teachings will receive 'a hundredfold *in this life* and the next.' Then I suddenly realized that God's way of living is meant to make my own life happier right *now*!"

"I'll say!" said Fred. "Going the extra mile gives me the satisfaction of a job well done, satisfied customers, and lots of referrals."

George was not sure that this was exactly what Jesus had in mind when he said that, but he had to admire the way that Fred took it seriously and saw a meaning in it for his own life. George thought about taking on more of this attitude when he was helping customers at Western Auto.

In addition to these personal insights into how to live the Gospel, George and the others also received more formal instruction in Catholic beliefs and practices. Using a book that Sister Janet had selected on the Catholic faith, George and the others learned about the Mass, sacraments, Catholic doctrines, Christian morality, and parish life.

Sister Janet had been right, George concluded, when she said it was a good thing you don't have to know *everything* about the Catholic Church to become a full member.

"I'm glad we don't have to take an exam on all this when the course is over!" George chimed in after a particularly heavy teaching session.

In addition to the weekly meetings, about once a month George and the other catechumens attended ten-thirty Mass on Sunday. They stayed until just after the homily. Then the priest blessed them with the prayer of exorcism, and they went with their sponsors to the rectory for brunch and a discussion of how they could see the readings applying to their own lives.

"The first part of the Mass used to be called the Mass of the catechumens," explained Father Mike one Sunday as they sat around sipping coffee beneath the pictures of laughing Jesus and Pope John XXIII. "Today we call it the Liturgy of the Word, but in the RCIA program we still follow the ancient practice of introducing catechumens to Catholic worship by allowing them to experience and reflect on just the first part of what we do every Sunday."

"I enjoy these small group sessions on our own," said Phil, "but what would happen if we stayed till the end of Mass?"

"These days, nothing," said Father Mike, "as you know from having gone to Mass with your family for some time now. But in the old days catechumens were not allowed to attend the Liturgy of the Eucharist, which used to be called the Mass of the Faithful. Only those who were baptized members of the Church could stay for the memorial of the Last Supper and Holy Communion. Then, like today, that part of the liturgy is the time when the Church calls the faithful to renew their commitment to live a sacrificial life, as Christ did. But since catechumens haven't made that public commitment yet, it's a little inappropriate for them to celebrate that part of the liturgy."

"That prayer about exorcism kind of gives me the heebie-jeebies," said George. "Does the Church *really* think we're possessed by the *devil* until we're baptized?"

Father Mike laughed. "Don't worry, George. We're not expecting any scenes like those in *The Exorcist!* In a prayer of exorcism, such as the one Father Henry used today, we ask God to protect you from all evil as you move closer to your Baptism. The way I look at it, we all have a bit of the devil in us unless we're perfect saints! These special prayers for catechumens remind us that we always need God's help to resist temptations that we might have succumbed to in the past."

By the following February, this lengthy part of the RCIA program was almost over. During the final weeks, the parish gave the candidates the Nicene Creed and the Lord's Prayer in special ceremonies, which marked the end of this phase of catechetical instruction. In these rites of presentation, they had been asked to receive two important symbols of the Church's faith, anticipating the day when they would personally profess their own faith in Christ. Now with this behind them, the group was about to begin a shorter but more intensive period of preparation.

"Most people are aware," said Sister Janet at their final evening meeting, "that in the Church Lent is a time for reflecting on what we'd like to improve in ourselves. What many people don't know, though, is what you are going to learn firsthand — that Lent originated from the catechumenate in the early centuries of Christianity. *Penitence,* or *repentance,* means the same as conversion, or change of mind and heart. The time has come, for those of you who are catechumens, to complete your conversion from what you were to what you will be when you accept Baptism in the Catholic Church."

"But what about those of us who were already baptized?" asked Phil. "Father Mike said we would not be baptized again."

"That's right, you won't be baptized. But the RCIA is a kind of baptismal process, or immersion, in the Church's life and the life of God. That's why we've invited you to join the others in this program.

"Your insight is right, though. The special ceremonies of Lent are really not intended for the unbaptized, so you and the others who were baptized in the Christian faith, even if it was in another church, won't be participating in them as fully as George, Kathy, and Arlene. In the Catholic Church, though, all who attend are invited to enter into the spirit of these rites as a reminder of their baptismal commitment to God. And, of course, since you all have been with us in the RCIA program this year, that invitation is especially extended to you. You and your families will have a place reserved for you between the catechumens and the rest of the congregation."

❄ ❄ ❄

On the first Sunday of Lent, the official catechumens from St. Anne's were asked to participate in the rite of election at the diocese's cathedral, along with the other catechumens in the diocese. Bishop Anzaro could not be present for all their baptisms, so he had designated this Sunday as the day when he could formally meet with all those who were about to join the Church.

"As the chief pastor in the diocese," said the bishop, "I personally welcome you all into the Catholic communion."

One by one the candidates for Baptism stepped forward with their sponsors, who from now on would be their godparents. A voice called out George's name. Father Mike followed George as he walked up to the bishop and they took their places among the others.

"And now I ask all those of you who are godparents, are the candidates ready to be baptized when Easter draws near?" The godparents nodded and assured the bishop that their charges were indeed ready.

"May I please see the names," Bishop Anzaro said and turned to a priest nearby. The priest handed him a scroll inscribed with the names of all the candidates. The bishop looked it over and then nodded, giving his approval to everyone on the list. He asked everyone in the cathedral to pray for those who were about to begin the solemn preparation for Baptism during Lent.

As the congregation prayed, Father Mike put his hand on George's shoulder. George glanced around and noticed that the other godparents had done the same. His stomach felt kind of fluttery and jumpy with excitement. He was glad Mike was there; it really was sort of like having an older brother around to help you out. George hoped and prayed that all the other candidates felt the warmth and acceptance that he felt.

❈ ❈ ❈

"So how does it feel to be among the 'elect,' George?" Father Mike asked his passenger as he eased his rusty Oldsmobile onto the freeway. Its powerful V-eight engine switched gears with ease and grace as it hauled them speedily into the flow of traffic.

"I'm not sure what I'm feeling," admitted George. "It feels sort of weird and good at the same time. It sure is different, though."

George found the following weeks in St. Anne's parish to be especially significant as he and the other catechumens worked at their initiation into the Church. On three of the Sundays in Lent, the candidates took part in special rites that occurred during Mass between the Liturgy of the Word and the Liturgy of the Eucharist. During these *scrutinies,* as they were called, the celebrant asked the candidates to examine their lives and motives for becoming Christians. He also asked the godparents to reflect on the readiness of the candidates for Baptism, and to do all they could to help during the initiates' final weeks of preparation.

The others in the RCIA program who had been previously baptized were also present for the scrutinies. As Phil, Lucy and Ralph, Frank and Henrietta got ready to return to full membership in the Church, these rites for the baptismal candidates helped them deepen their appreciation for their own Baptism. The members of the parish who attended these special Masses also found that they were growing in their understanding of the Christian life as they saw what it meant to the people in the program.

During Holy Week, three brief ceremonies concluded the adult candidates' preparation for Baptism — they recited the Nicene Creed, received a blessing on their ears and mouths, and then the local pastor anointed them with the oil of catechumens.

The next and final event they all awaited was their formal reception into the Church on Holy Saturday, the vigil of Easter.

❈ ❈ ❈

"Are you ready, George?"

Father Mike had just stopped by the parlor in the rectory where the RCIA group had spent so many evenings together preparing for this event. George was surprised to see his friend dressed in his full liturgical vestments. Just a few minutes before, they all had finished a formal dinner that Father Henry hosted each year for the catechumens and their sponsors.

"Sure thing! I'm ready!" proclaimed George as he combed his hair. "Let's get this show on the road!"

The others smiled and laughed a bit. George wondered to himself if he shouldn't say such light things before such a solemn occasion.

Sister Janet reviewed with them the final details of the ceremony that would begin at ten o'clock.

"George, you and Kathy and Arlene will be baptized tonight, so you'll be sitting together with your godparents. Father Mike, you'll be at the altar with Father Henry, but you know when to come down and stand by George."

"All right. I'll see you all in a little while at the church entrance." With that, Mike waved good-bye and Sister Janet continued.

"Phil, you've already been baptized, but since you were not confirmed in the Catholic Church, you'll be celebrating your Confirmation when the others are confirmed after their Baptism, just as we rehearsed last week.

"Lucy and Ralph, Frank and Henrietta, you'll be seated with your families just across the aisle from the others, and you'll renew your baptismal promises with the congregation right after the others are baptized and confirmed. We do this every year at Easter time, but it's been awhile since you did it, so really, you all have something important to celebrate tonight."

"Father Mike said there would also be some children being baptized this Easter. Are they here tonight?" asked Kathy.

"No, in some parishes they are," replied Sister Janet. "But we feel that it is better to celebrate their Baptism at the Mass in the morning. Many of the infants come from families with other young children, and a long ceremony late at night would be hard for them to sit through. Besides, this way the parishioners attending the morning Mass can also celebrate the Baptism of new members into the Church."

"But babies who are baptized could not have gone through the same process we did," observed Kathy.

"You're absolutely right," answered Sister Janet. "But during the six weeks of Lent their parents and godparents have been participating in a program preparing for their children's Baptism. Those parents will be the primary catechists of their own children as they grow up in a Catholic home, so it's important that they learn how to do it. The parents also get support from one another, making friends with other members of the parish who have small children just as they do. It's a wonderful community-building program in that respect. They also learn about our preschool religious education program and receive advice on how to help their children grow in the faith at home. It's another way we try to strengthen Christian family life, in addition to the other programs and activities we offer in the parish."

"But I heard that Catholic children are supposed to be baptized soon after they are born," said Kathy. "Do you mean that infants have to wait each year till Easter for their Baptism?"

"Oh, no. We conduct the Baptism preparation program for parents about four times a year here in St. Anne's, and their children are baptized at a Sunday liturgy right after that. Sometimes the babies aren't even born yet when the moms and dads are coming to the program! And, of course, we also have private Baptisms for children, if necessary. But we encourage all our parents to participate in the Sunday Baptisms, since it makes for a much more communal celebration. And that's what Baptism is all about — joining the Christian community."

"Say, isn't it about time *we* joined the Christian community over at the church?" interrupted Frank, looking at his watch.

"You're right! Father Henry will be lighting the Easter fire in a few minutes. But don't worry. Your places are being held for you. And I'm sure they won't start without us!"

The evening air was nippy, with the wind sending a peaceful rustle through the maple trees in front of church on this moonless night. The small group of catechumens made their way to the semicircle that surrounded the small fire in a brazier next to Father Henry.

"In ancient times," began the pastor, "the Easter fire was a big bonfire that announced the start of spring and the return of warmth to the land. For Christians it came to symbolize the love of God and the warmth we all experience as members of the Christian family as a whole. Out of the fire of God's love the sun and stars and all good things that have life were created. And out of that same divine fire and into our world came Jesus, the light of God in a world of darkness. Tonight we remember this as we light the Easter candle, which will burn in our church tonight and throughout the Easter season."

Father Henry blessed and lit the large candle. He then carried it into the vestibule of the darkened church, leading the procession of catechumens and their sponsors.

"Christ our light!" Father Mike proclaimed.

"Thanks be to God!" everyone in the church responded.

Twice more, once in the middle of the church and then in front of the altar, the priest and people sang their affirmation of Christ as the light of their lives.

From the Easter candle, Deacon John then lit a taper and passed the light to the altar boys who went down the center aisle, stopping at each pew to spread the light throughout the church. George looked back and was amazed to see how much light one candle could give when it was shared with others.

Father Henry explained: "Through our Baptism the light of Christ has been passed to each one of us. Jesus, the Light of the World, told his disciples, 'You are the light of the world.' Tonight we see how bright our world can be if we keep our faith burning brightly and pass it on to others. Let us recall now how God's light came into the world, through creation, through the history of God's people in Israel, and through God's Son, Jesus."

The lectors and celebrant read more from the Bible than George had ever heard in a single church service. He heard about the beginning of the world, the sacrifice of Abraham, and the Exodus of the Israelites from Egypt. Then the second lector read about promises revealed through the prophets and the meaning of Christ's Resurrection. Finally, Father Henry read the exciting story about the first Easter morning.

Although George pretty much knew the story, the quiet of the night, the glow of the candles, and the faces of the people around him listening intently made the story seem like it was all happening right that moment, especially inside of him.

When he finished reading, Father Henry asked everyone to pray for those who were about to be baptized. He, of course, asked for God's blessings, but then also started reading off a list of saints. George had heard about a litany before, but this was the first time that he realized how seriously Catholics take their belief that the Church includes not only the faithful on earth but also the blessed in heaven.

The names of the many saints flowed forth from Father Henry's lips and each time the people responded, "Pray for us." George heard familiar names like Francis and Theresa, but also hard-to-pronounce names like Perpetua and Athanasius. It dawned on him that these were some of the same people displayed in the pictures above the sofa in the rectory.

Father Henry blessed the baptismal water and approached the candidates, asking them to rise. "Do you reject Satan, and all his works and empty promises?" Father asked.

"I do," they answered together.

Father Henry motioned to those to be baptized so they would step closer to the baptismal font. He then anointed each of them, saying, "We anoint you with the oil of salvation in the name of Christ our Savior. May he strengthen you with his power...."

At this point, Father Mike walked over to George to stand beside him as godparent.

Father Henry baptized Arlene first, and then it was George's turn.

"George, do you believe in God, the Father Almighty, Creator of heaven and earth?"

"I do," he replied.

"Do you believe in Jesus Christ, his only Son, our Lord, who was born of the Virgin Mary, was crucified, died, and was buried, rose from the dead, and is now seated at the right hand of the Father?"

"I do."

"Do you believe in the Holy Spirit, the holy catholic Church, the communion of saints, the forgiveness of sins, the resurrection of the body, and life everlasting?"

"I do."

With that, Father Henry invited George to step up to the baptismal font, from which he took some water and poured it over George's head, saying, "George, I baptize you in the name of the Father, and of the Son, and of the Holy Spirit."

It was all very real, and yet to George it seemed to happen in slow motion — like one of those "my life flashed before my eyes" moments. He felt an inner shift — like the shape of the letter "Z" he made when downshifting from third to second gear to give his car's engine more power.

Like the letter "Z," George had been moving forward in one direction. But meeting and getting to know Mike and going through RCIA had been like a step across and backward in time to where George thought about who he really was, what he really wanted, and who he wanted to be remembered as when he left this world.

"We are in the world but not of it," Sister Janet had once said, commenting on a Scripture reading.

And so on this cold evening on the cusp of spring, George Mays shifted to the last line that formed that "Z." It was the line that moved parallel to the first, yet was new and different just as his life was now new and different even though he was still George Mays, assistant manager of the Western Auto store.

After they dried themselves off, each of the newly baptized people donned a white garment over their clothes, signifying their spiritual rebirth into the life of Christ.

Each godparent gave a lit candle to the newest members of the Church as Father Henry continued speaking: "You have been enlightened by Christ. Walk always as children of the Light and keep the flame of faith alive in your hearts. When the Lord comes, may you go out to meet him with all the saints in the heavenly kingdom."

Next, Father Henry invited Phil to join the newly baptized for the ceremony of Confirmation. Again, after inviting everyone in the church to join him in praying for the candidates, he continued aloud: "All-powerful God, Father of our Lord Jesus Christ, by water and the Holy Spirit you freed your sons and daughters from sin and gave them new life. Send your Holy Spirit upon them to be their helper and guide. Give them the spirit of wisdom and under-standing, the spirit of right judgment and courage, the spirit of knowledge and reverence. Fill them with wonder and awe in your presence. We ask you this through Christ our Lord."

Approaching each of the candidates, the pastor then made the sign of the cross on each of their foreheads with chrism oil, saying, "Be sealed with the Holy Spirit, the Gift of the Father."

"Amen," they all responded.

"Peace be with you."

"And also with you," they all said.

So *this* was peace, George thought; and he knew that it was good.

Finally, with the Confirmations completed, Father Henry walked to the center to face the congregation and said, "Our new brothers and sisters in Christ have just witnessed to their faith in God and their acceptance of the beliefs of the Catholic Church. We also have with us this evening some brothers and sisters who are returning to the Church, and at this time I would like to invite them to step forward with their families and friends."

When Lucy and Ralph, Frank and Henrietta, and those who had come with them had taken their places, the pastor continued: "Spring is a time of renewal for nature, and Easter is a time of renewal for our spirits. For this reason the liturgy calls us to renew our commitment to God and the Church by remaking the promises of our Baptism."

Father Henry then went through the baptismal vows, while the whole assembly stood and repeated their assent to each of them.

"And now," he went on, "let us show our approval and appreciation for our sisters and brothers who have joined or rejoined our family tonight."

When George heard the applause, he felt a little awkward, wondering if he should take a bow or something besides just standing there. But before he could think of anything, he heard Father Henry saying, "Peace be with you."

"And also with you," came the response from the congregation.

"Let us now share with one another a sign of God's peace."

It took awhile to get through all the hugging and handshaking that followed, but at the end of it George and the other catechumens found themselves back in the front pews of the church as the assembly prepared to continue with the liturgy.

Although George and the others had attended Masses before, this one was special. Some of the sponsors led the general intercessions, praying for the newly baptized at St. Anne's and at all the Catholic churches around the world. Then some of the catechumens carried the gifts of bread and wine up to the altar. Something else was also special for the newly baptized and confirmed, and for the newly reunited members of the Church. Not only did they receive Communion for the first time (or the first time in many years) but they were invited up to the altar to receive the sacrament of Christ's body and blood. As he received the consecrated bread and the chalice of wine, George felt he understood more than ever before why they call this the sacrament of Christian unity. He experienced a sense of oneness with Christ that up till now he had only heard about. It was like…what was it like? George could not quite place the feeling at first. It was something he had felt before…but when?

Sitting with his eyes closed after he returned to the pew, George meditated on the feeling, searching his memory for when he had felt this before. *When was it?* It was so familiar, yet elusive.

When he remembered, he was glad he had his eyes closed. It had happened ten years earlier…in a hospital room where he sat beside his brother's bed in the cancer ward. The family thought Herm would have a few more months, but he'd taken an unexpected turn for the worse. Herm had taught George all about working on V-eights, straight sixes, slant sixes. In the quiet hospital room that afternoon, George thought Herm was sleeping but then felt a tap on his arm. Herm motioned for his brother to come closer and said, "Keep up your good work on my car. I expect to be able to drive it when I'm outa here." Herm clasped George's hand and said, "I love you…." Then Herm closed his eyes and died.

As the flutist and organist wrapped up the final notes of the meditation hymn at St. Anne's, tears welled in George's closed eyes. Now he remembered; that's what the moment felt like.

George took a deep breath and suddenly remembered something else as he watched Father Henry and Father Mike wiping out their gleaming chalices up at the altar. George smiled, remembering the chrome on Herm's old car — a gas-guzzling behemoth of an automobile whose front end would arrive home half a block before its driver did. And George thanked God for Herm, Father Mike, and their two Oldsmobiles.

Making a Deal With the Holy Spirit

(Confirmation)

Kevin scanned the parish hall to see how many of his friends from the youth group had come to the Confirmation meeting. He squirmed on the metal folding chair. Between the heads of some parents he spotted friends five rows back — Alan, David, Pete, and Leroy — goofing off as usual. In chairs near them sat Rachel, Laura, and Amy. The girls bent over and huddled among themselves as Amy's bangled and braceleted arms clinked and clacked to illustrate her speech with sweeping gestures.

Kevin watched her. He wondered if her hair was naturally curly. He wondered what she saw in stuck-up Michael Marcovich. He wondered if it was worth a try to ask her out.

"Staring at Amy again?"

Kevin jumped, startled by his friend's voice. "Cut it out, Eric," he pleaded. "She's not so hot. If you really want to know, I was looking for you. I thought you'd be sitting closer to the back."

"I would," said Eric, "except my dad forgot his glasses and made us sit in front."

"Hi there, Eric," said Kevin's mother.

"Hi, Mrs. Whalen."

"I think you'd better get back to your seat. It looks like the meeting is about to begin," she said.

Mr. Hanlon stood at the podium, bending over the microphone and flicking it with his middle finger. "Is this thing on?" he asked. "Testing, testing...."

Feedback screeched from the speakers on the stage. Many parents held their hands over their ears. A startled baby began crying. One of the other teachers dashed backstage to check the public address system controls. Then, with the problem remedied, Mr. Hanlon continued.

"I'd like to welcome all the young people who are here with their parents this evening. As the parish director of religious education, I'm here tonight to introduce you to the team who will be working with you and your folks in this year's Confirmation preparation program. Chuck and Angela Petruzzo are the directors of the youth group that meets here in this hall every week. Mrs. Carter over there is the coordinator for our junior and senior high religious education programs. And, of course, you all know Father Anthony Seroka who, besides being our pastor, is on the bishop's committee for youth ministry in our diocese.

"Ever since Father Seroka came to Blessed Trinity Parish, he has made a special effort to reach out to our young people, since they are the future of the Church. Our youth group, the young people's choir, the many activities that our kids are engaged in all over the parish, and this Confirmation program owe a lot to his constant efforts to involve kids and young adults in the life of the Church. Both they and we who have children of our own have gotten an awful lot from him in the few years that he's been with us. Father Tony, would you start us off tonight?"

Father Tony walked casually to the lectern and placed his hands in his pockets. "Thank you, Jim," he said. "It's nice to hear those compliments, but I give a lot of credit for what goes on here to the Holy Spirit. I really mean that. There's no way that one person could do all the things I'm sometimes given credit for."

He looked intently at a group of parents in the front row, saying, "If I have any personal gift, I would say it's the gift of listening. I just listen to what kids are saying, what parents are saying, what the elderly and shut-ins in our parish are saying....I listen to all of that, and I listen to what I hear the Holy Spirit saying about how good it is for people to get together to sing and praise the Lord and to help those who have no one else to help them. Then I just go around asking people if they'd like to get together to do this or that.

"More often than not, when I do that, something good comes of it. I get the inspiration, as it were, from the Holy Spirit. Then I let the Spirit provide the energy to keep the good things that have started going and growing. And that power to do good things for

29

other people is a way that we ourselves become enriched. That, too, is a gift that comes from the Holy Spirit.

"I suppose I learned the most about the work of the Holy Spirit years ago when I first became involved with charismatic renewal in the Church. We have a charismatic prayer group in our parish which some of our young people are involved with. But that style of prayer is not for everybody, and I don't personally think that God needs everyone to pray in tongues and do the other dramatic sorts of things that appeal to charismatics. But God *does* want everyone to be filled with the Spirit — to live the life of the Spirit — because — well, you find out after a while that that's the only way to live. It's the only way that life really seems worthwhile.

"You know, at the very beginning, living in the Holy Spirit was not called Christianity. It wasn't even called the Catholic Church. Those names weren't invented until later. In the beginning, it was simply called The Way, meaning the way of Jesus, the way of God, the right way and the best way to live. Jesus said, 'I am the way and the truth and the life,' and he showed his disciples the true way to live.

"The Scriptures tell us, though, that after Jesus' Resurrection and Ascension something was missing from the disciples' lives. They knew the way Jesus wanted them to live, but somehow they lacked the power to do it.

"Then, on the Solemnity of Pentecost, God sent the Holy Spirit to them, and their lives changed. They were like people on fire. They burned with the desire to bring the good news about Jesus and his way of life to others. They brought others into their community through Baptism, and they prayed that their new brothers and sisters would receive the Spirit of Jesus. They even touched them as they prayed, in order to communicate the Spirit to them.

"As time went on the community grew larger, and those first Christians initiated others into the life of Jesus. The followers of Jesus became known as a church or religious assembly, and Saint Paul in his letters called it the Body of Christ, since it was a body of believers who were filled with the spirit of Jesus. From that day to this, we have been assisting people who want to be initiated into the life of the Church through Baptism, prayer, and the laying on of hands.

"Through the centuries, however, the Church has made some changes in how this is done. An anointing with holy oil, or chrism, was added to symbolize the pouring of the Holy Spirit on the baptized. This anointing and the laying on of hands was separated by a few years from the Baptism of infants so that their bishop could personally confirm them. That is why today we prepare young people for Confirmation a number of years after their infant Baptism.

"Most of you parents, I'll bet, were probably confirmed sometime during grade school; and there are a lot of places around the country where that's still the practice. But the bishops in every country have the pastoral authority to adapt the traditional practice to the changing needs of their dioceses. That's why our own bishop, Robert Knowles, thought it would be better to postpone Confirmation until the junior high or high school years.

"There are a couple of important reasons for this. The main one is to help young people make a more mature decision about affirming their own Baptism and committing themselves to the life of Christ as it is lived in the Catholic Church. Bishop Knowles sees that in today's world, those who are baptized as infants are bombarded with many different values and lifestyle options in their teen years. He wanted to give young people a special opportunity to reflect on the baptismal promises their parents and godparents made for them. When he consulted the youth ministry leaders in the diocese, he found that almost all of them agreed with him.

"That's why, in our diocese now, teenagers wait until eighth or ninth grade before asking to be confirmed in the Church. They can, however, postpone their Confirmation indefinitely until they are ready to affirm and commit to the full responsibility of being a Catholic in today's world. The bishop realizes that given this freedom, some young people may not choose to be confirmed until they are much older or, in rare cases, they may never choose to be confirmed. But the bishop feels that confirming people when they are ready to assume adult responsibilities in the Church is better than confirming them when they are children who do not fully understand the commitment they are making.

"And that brings up the second reason for waiting to confirm young people until they are a little older. Confirmation, we can say, is both a Confirmation of Baptism and an affirmation of the new life that Christ brings to us. Bishop Knowles acts on behalf of all the people in the diocese when he confirms and completes each person's initiation into the Christian life. All of the candidates, acting on their own behalf, affirm and accept the new life into which we initiated them as children.

"But accepting that new life as a young adult also means accepting the responsibilities of that life. You don't move into marriage or the priesthood without accepting new responsibilities. In the past it was often the case that the Church confirmed children without those children understanding and freely accepting adult responsibilities in the Church. They *couldn't, they were just children.* Their lives after Confirmation weren't any different than they were before. But our bishop and our youth ministry leaders believe Confirmation ought to introduce young people to the responsibilities of adult Christian life.

"Here in Blessed Trinity Parish we try to put that idea into practice by requiring each person who steps forward for Confirmation to get involved in some work of service for at least one year. It may be a service to the parish or a service to individuals who need some particular help in their lives. We encourage them to continue in that service, or to move into new ones as they get older, so they can experience the rewards of sharing themselves with others.

"Mrs. Carter, though, is the person who really knows all about that aspect of the Confirmation program. So at this point I'll turn the microphone over to her."

"Thank you, Father Tony," said Mrs. Carter as she put on her glasses. "Actually, there are two parts to our preparation program for Confirmation. The first is devoted to helping young people decide whether this is the right time to enter Christian adulthood. It begins with these meetings so they and their parents can better understand what Confirmation is all about. During the next few weeks, you will discern whether you're ready to request Confirmation this year or would rather wait to take this important step.

"Then we will have a retreat day, or 'Spirit Day,' as we call it. On Spirit Day the teens will gather with our youth ministry team to pray together and reflect on what their Confirmation will mean to them personally."

Eric leaned over to Kevin and whispered, "But what about the kids who *don't* choose Confirmation? Do they have to go to the retreat too?"

"I don't know," said Kevin. "Maybe you can ask that question later."

Mrs. Carter continued, "The second part of the program also

begins on Spirit Day. We have other kids as well as adults describe the various needs in our parish and in our city, and what ministering to those needs have meant to them. Some of them are involved in service to the parish, singing or helping in other ways with weekend worship, taking care of the buildings and grounds, working in our religious education programs, and programs of that sort. The others are involved in service to individuals — shut-ins, the elderly, people in hospitals and nursing homes, children who need help with schoolwork. Our speakers explain to them what the needs are, what kind of time commitment is required to meet those needs, and the rewards experienced in answering those needs.

"During the week before Confirmation, then, the teens, with their parents' help, select which ministry they want to serve in during the coming year. At the Confirmation ceremony itself, as you know if you've been to one already, the parish recognizes and applauds the young people's choices to enter the adult life of the Church. You'll be hearing more about that, however, as time goes on. For right now, though, are there any questions about anything that's been said tonight?"

Then Eric's father raised his hand and asked, "What if a kid chooses not to be confirmed at this time or has already been confirmed? Will they still go through the Spirit Day and other preparations?"

"Yes, they will," Mrs. Carter said. "Spirit Day is not just a day of preparation for the actual Confirmation ceremony, it will be a valuable experience for any Christian wanting to learn more about living a life of service to God and neighbor."

When it was all over, Kevin's mother turned to him and asked, "Well, what do you think?"

"I don't know…I guess it's all right. Did you have to go through all this when you were confirmed?"

"When I was younger, it was more like what Father Tony said. In some ways it was easier, and in some ways it was harder."

"How so?"

"Well, I'd say it was easier because all the kids in my grade got confirmed without having to volunteer for anything. But it was also harder because I had to wait until I was a grownup to learn how much richer life can be when you care for other people besides yourself and your family."

"What do you mean?" Eric leaned over and asked.

"Oh, you'll find out," said Mrs. Whalen. "Say, would you mind finding some of your friends and talking for a while? I have to catch Mrs. Hofstadter before she leaves. I want to ask her about the next meeting of our single parents' group."

❄ ❄ ❄

"That was a fine supper, Kevin. Wasn't it, Melissa?" said Mrs. Whalen as she wiped her mouth with her napkin.

"Not as good as the ones I make!" announced Kevin's younger sister.

"You got a head start on helping me in the kitchen when you were a little girl," their mother said, "but Kevin's been catching up with you the past few years. Anyhow, this way the two of you can take turns at cooking and cleaning up so you don't have to face the same chores every week."

"I'm getting to be a pretty good chef, ain't I, Mom?" said Kevin, grinning at his sister.

"*Please* don't say 'ain't,' Kevin. You know I don't like that. But yes, you sure are getting to be a good chef. I really appreciate it the way you both help out with the housework and the meals, especially on a night like tonight when I have a meeting to attend. I just wouldn't have time, otherwise."

"Well, I'm out some nights too," said Kevin, "going to Junior Achievement and the youth group. And this week we have that Confirmation meeting again."

"*Another* one!" said Melissa. "It sure sounds like a big deal, this getting confirmed stuff. You get to go to all these meetings, and I'm always stuck at home with doing dishes or laundry with one of you, or a baby-sitter. I hate that!"

"Maybe next year, when you're a little older," said Mrs. Whalen. "Right now I still feel safer when you're not home by yourself at night."

"Can I put the dishes off till later?" asked Melissa. "I want to call Rory first."

"You just saw her today at school," objected Kevin.

"Sure you can," Mrs. Whalen overrode his objection. "Just make sure to put the leftovers in the refrigerator before you call and have the kitchen cleaned up by the time I get back from my meeting."

Kevin helped clear the table, then rejoined his mother at the table while she made herself a cup of instant coffee.

"Our life sure isn't dull, is it?" sighed Mrs. Whalen. "I was afraid it might be after your father left."

"Are you still mad him, Mom?"

"Oh, I guess I sometimes am, but it's not as bad as it was at first. You really helped out a lot back then. Your sister couldn't be very helpful at her age then. I felt embarrassed sometimes, especially when you were around and I'd start crying. But the people in our single parents' group helped me learn how to accept my feelings and share them with others."

Kevin's mother traced the flowers in the tablecloth with her finger, gazing at them absent-mindedly. "And you've become a really good listener. I think we've all grown a lot these past two years."

"Is that why you go to these meetings every week, to talk about how you feel?" Kevin asked.

"Well, for that, and also because now I figure it's my turn to help other people too — the way others helped me when I needed it."

"What do they *do* at the meetings?"

"Well, this one's a training meeting. It's for people in the parish who want to learn to help others through pastoral counseling. We learn how to listen to people better and help them work out their problems. Sometimes people are recently divorced or widowed or have lost a job or are having trouble in their families. This meeting will be about learning how to be a real neighbor to people. We also learn how to spot the kinds of problems that people might need professional help with and then refer them to others who can help them even more."

"What kinds of problems?"

"Things like alcoholism, drug problems, child or spouse battering, teenage pregnancies, mental illness — you name it. A year ago I thought *I* was the only one with problems! But I've realized that there are *lots* of people right here in our own parish who need help with things they can't cope with alone. And they don't have to cope with them alone if people reach out to help them the way they reached out to help us."

"I guess we're pretty lucky, huh?"

"Sure, we're lucky. I'm lucky that your father and I could work things out with the alimony until I found a job. And you're lucky that your Uncle Charles invited you to his place at the beach the past two summers. But it wasn't just luck, Kevin. There were also a lot of people who went out of their way to help us. That didn't happen just by luck. It meant a lot of time and effort on their part."

"Is that why you're doing this pastoral helping thing?"

"Yes, but there are lots of other things to do in our parish besides help people in trouble. You heard Father Seroka talk last week about the charismatic prayer group. Well, there's that, a Cursillo group, and a Marriage Encounter group, Bible study groups, and a rosary group. There are all the people who work in the religious education programs from preschool to adult ed. There's the RCIA team and the youth ministry. And there's all the people who help plan the liturgies, set up for the Masses, serve at the altar, and sing in the choir. And don't forget the Men's Society and the Women's Sodality; some of their members have belonged to those clubs for over twenty-five years! They organize the monthly parish breakfasts and the weekly suppers at the rectory. The list just goes on and on."

"Why do people do all those things? Do they get paid?"

"I guess you'd say they get paid, but not with money. It's like when you make the supper for us. What do you get paid?"

"Well, it depends on whether I mess up and burn the meat or something," said Kevin.

"Well, when you *don't* burn the meat or something and everything turns out good; *then* what do you get paid?" asked Mrs. Whalen.

"I guess I feel good about it," he replied.

"Exactly. You get paid something that money can't buy. I guess you could call it happiness. But it's a grown-up sort of happiness. The kind you get when you've helped people and you can see that you've made their lives a little happier. You get paid when you see their eyes brighten up and smiles on their faces. You get paid in friendship; you know more people, and they know you."

"Is that why we have to do this service thing for Confirmation?"

"Yes, I think that's it. Father Seroka and Mrs. Carter talked about it being a lesson in responsibility. But I personally think the real reason for it is happiness. You know what you sometimes hear at Christmas; that it's more blessed to give than to receive? Well, as you get older, you discover that that's true the whole year-round. It takes some people a long time to learn that. I'm glad for you that you're learning it when you're young."

"Hey, Mom, look at the clock! It's almost time for your meeting."

"You're right. I've got to hurry. What's on your agenda for tonight?"

"I'm going to try making some funnel cakes like they have at the fair and the parish picnic. I got a recipe for it from Eric's mom. Do we have enough Crisco for me to deep-fry stuff?"

"That's kind of dangerous — hot grease and no adult supervision."

"Oh, I'll get Eric to help me."

"How so?"

"Before you came home he asked me if I would help him with his homework. I said he could come over after supper."

Mrs. Whalen put her hands on her hips and looked seriously at her son. "Well, I do like you to ask permission to have your friends over. But I like it even more that you're doing what we were just talking about."

"What's that?"

"Helping people and being friends. It's what makes us happy."

"Aw, Mom!"

"Now give me a hug, and I'll be off."

❋ ❋ ❋

Near the old stove in the basement Eric said, "I guess that does it," as he turned off the deep fryer.

"Yeah, these were really good," said Kevin as he popped a piece of funnel cake into his mouth. A dusting of powdered sugar rested on his cheek. "They taste better than the ones at the county fair or the school picnic."

"Yeah," said Eric. "My mom says the fairs use some sort of premixed stuff with all kinds of chemicals in it, but this way you make the batter fresh and the cakes taste really good."

"We'd better move the table back over in the corner where we got it from," said Kevin.

As Kevin huffed and puffed to help move the heavy oak table, Eric said, "You know what you should put in the spot we moved it from? A weightlifting bench and set of weights for working out."

"I'm not really into that the way you are, Eric. I'd rather work on my models."

"Yeah, but if you worked out every day you could move this table by yourself!" said Eric as the two boys lowered the table back into its original spot. They walked toward the stairs.

"Hey, why should I go through all that effort when I can just call you up to help me?" Kevin said and gave his friend a harmless shove, but the more muscular boy easily kept his balance. "That's what friends are for, right?"

"Now don't go taking advantage of me!" said Eric, with a smirk. "I wouldn't do this for everybody."

"Why not?" asked Kevin as they walked up the basement stairs.

"Because before you know it, everybody'll be asking you for favors. You got to look out for yourself first."

Kevin tried to think of a quick comeback but couldn't. "What did you bring for homework?" he asked changing the subject.

❄ ❄ ❄

In the following weeks Kevin and his mother attended the other Confirmation program meetings. At the second meeting Mr. Hanlon, the religious education director, talked more about the history of Confirmation and how it was related to Baptism. He showed a film that explained the theology of the sacrament in terms of personal growth and community spirit.

Mr. and Mrs. Petruzzo from the youth group led the meeting after that. They talked about the spiritual needs of young people and how important it is to keep growing in relationship to God and others. Some other adults came in and told about how they had gone through an adult conversion that made prayer and the Scriptures come alive for them. They also told about how they now had a personal relationship with Jesus that they didn't have when they were younger.

Mr. Hanlon again led the fourth and final meeting in the evening series. This time he talked about sharing the life of God with people outside the Church through various kinds of social involvement. He showed a film about the U.S. bishops' Campaign for Human Development and the way that Catholics around the world help people help themselves out of poverty. In the discussion that followed, he emphasized how working for social justice grows naturally out of reading the Scriptures and responding to God's call to spiritual maturity.

"Boy, those meetings are a drag," complained Leroy over the lunch table at school the next day.

"Yeah, they're not like our youth group meetings. Those are fun," agreed Eric.

Leroy went on, directing his speech to Kevin, "Do you really believe all that stuff about talking to God and everything?"

"I don't know," responded Kevin as he looked deeply into his tuna fish sandwich. He thought the meetings were interesting but hesitated to admit it to his friends.

"Well, Whalen, what do you think?" pressed Leroy.

"They're OK," Kevin managed to say.

"For *real*? Are you *kidding*?" Eric said. "It's just a bunch of stories, though, like Noah and the Flood and all that."

"Yeah, really," Leroy seconded.

Silence hung like fog between Kevin and his friends. Eric wadded up his paper lunch bag and tossed it, basketball style, toward the trash bin. The bag hit the rim and bounced onto the floor. "Phooey," Eric said and turned back to the table. "I can't believe you *like* those boring meetings. It's just another plot by parents and teachers to get us to do everything they want us to do."

Kevin felt his face getting hot as he got increasingly angry with his friend. "Hey, wait a minute," objected Kevin. "You're supposed to *believe* that if you're going to be confirmed. I think so, anyway," he added, not wanting to start an argument.

"Who's going to be confirmed?" asked Leroy sarcastically, as though only ninety-pound weaklings got confirmed.

"Well, aren't you?" asked Kevin.

"Naw, I talked my way out of it. No way I'm gonna sign my life away for a year on one of those volunteer projects. I've got football now and basketball in the winter." Leroy had his mind made up.

"What about you, Eric?" Kevin asked.

"I really don't want to, either," his friend admitted.

"But you're both in the parish youth group, and that's religious...sort of," Kevin pointed out.

"Yeah, *sort of*," echoed Leroy, "but not *too* sort of."

"I can put up with a sermon now and then," said Eric, "but I could really do without them too."

"Then why stay in it?" Kevin asked.

"For the same reason half the guys are in it," Leroy interjected. "It's fun! Last winter we got to go skiing, and then there was that camping trip, and don't forget Rachel and Laura and Amy…."

"So you're not going to be confirmed then, either?" Kevin looked at Eric.

"I didn't say that."

"But you said you didn't want to be."

"What *I* want and what my *mother* wants are two different things."

"You mean she's making you do it?"

"Her and my dad. They said I had to or else no allowance."

"But that's not fair," protested Kevin.

"Hey, life's not fair," Eric said, looking wearily at his friend.

"What are you going to do for your service project?"

Eric didn't say anything, but instead fiddled around with the straw in his milk carton.

"Eric?" Kevin persisted.

"Can you keep a secret?" Eric finally asked.

"Sure."

Eric smiled as he whispered, "I'm not going to do nothin'."

"Oh, right; how are you going to get away with *that*?" Kevin scoffed.

"Well, the way I have it figured, I'll go ahead and sign up," said Eric, "but I don't *have* to do it."

"But that's not honest!"

"Where have you *been*, Whalen? Sure, this honest, nicey-nice stuff works in church and here at a Catholic school and at church picnics, but in the real world it's a whole different story. All you got to do is read the front page of a newspaper — marines selling military secrets to the Russians, people cheating one another out of money, guys making a fortune on selling drugs….Who's honest these days when money's involved? My dad's always saying that. My folks'll never know it if I don't go through with the service project. I'll just say I signed up for something that doesn't exist."

Kevin's irritation grew to a point where he almost felt like punching Eric. But then he felt Leroy glaring at him and remembered how easy it had been for muscular Eric to move the big table in the basement. "I don't know…" was all Kevin said.

"You don't have to *know* anything. Just keep cool," said Eric.

❄ ❄ ❄

Going on the Spirit Day retreat was a big step. It meant making a commitment to the Church and to service in the parish for at least one year. Leroy didn't show; Eric did.

"Hey, Kevin, how's it goin'?" Eric asked as he pulled up a folding chair alongside Kevin. Everything was normal in Eric's world.

"Hi" was all that Kevin could manage.

"I see that almost all of the girls are here…the good-looking ones anyway," said Eric. "I'll bet you're glad that Amy made it."

"Knock it off," said Kevin. "All you ever think of is girls."

"Well, why not? They're fun to think about and even more fun to go out with! A little weightlifting helps in that department too."

"So are you still going through with your plans?" asked Kevin.

"Sure, why not? I've figured out all the angles," Eric said as he glanced around the room, checking out who was and wasn't there.

"Except one," said Kevin with a flash of inspiration.

"What's that?"

"The girls."

"Huh?"

"I mean they'll figure out that you're not in on any of the service projects with them. They're not dumb. They'll talk to one another and realize you're bugging out. They're going to lose interest in you real fast." Kevin surprised himself with his tough-turkey talk.

Eric raised an eyebrow at Kevin. "Naw, they don't think that much. They just talk about hair and nails and soap operas. They just want a guy who'll show them a good time."

"You really think so?" said Eric.

"Hey, which one of us is the expert here? I go out two or three nights a week. That's more than *you* can say."

"Yeah, and then you come to *me* for help with your homework."

"That's the secret, kid. 'One hand washes the other,' my dad says. With your brains and my good looks, we can really go places."

"Sure, Eric."

"Hey, what did you put down for parish service?" asked Eric. "I left mine blank. I need some ideas. You know, something where the teachers won't miss me. What's a service that has a *lot* of kids in it?"

"Well, I put the youth group as my first choice. I'll bet everybody did, but we won't all get it, that's for sure. I also thought I'd sign up for helping out with the Sunday parish breakfasts. You only have to do it for a month, and I'm good in the kitchen." Kevin moved down his xeroxed sheet with a pencil. "For my third choice I put helping kids with their schoolwork. I figure if I can teach a dummy like you, I can teach anybody!"

"Watch out who you're calling 'dummy,' calculator brain!" joked Eric. "I didn't know you could sign up for things like that."

"It's something new my mother told me about. The parents' association organized it for the kids in grade school. You don't have to be a member of the parish to help out, but someone thought the Confirmation group might be a good place to find volunteers. Since not too many kids know about it, I figure I'd have a good chance of getting into that, if I don't get my first two picks."

"You smart guys really bug me," teased Eric. "You're always figuring out all the angles."

"You've got to if you don't want other people always telling you what to do," said Kevin, trying to drop his friend another hint.

The day started out with songs led by a few guitarists, and then the group settled down for a few words from Mrs. Carter. She directed the students to count off into six groups. The rest of the morning each group discussed questions presented by the adult leader at their table and then did some activities. Kevin didn't know the five other kids very well, but as the hours went by he realized he was relieved that Eric was babbling away in some other group on the other side of the room.

Kevin's group talked about their families, and where they lived, and why they had decided to receive the sacrament of Confirmation. They talked about what they liked and didn't like about the Church, and what they could do to make it better. Then they talked about Jesus and the Holy Spirit — a conversation that had its fair share of fits and starts. Kevin didn't know too much about the Holy Spirit and couldn't figure out what he was *supposed* to say.

"Now we're going to look at a parable," said Alan, the college student who was the group's leader. He handed out more xeroxed sheets, and everybody read about a sower who planted seeds and how the seeds grew differently depending on where they fell. "Now let's make this into a skit," said Alan. The group groaned and laughed at the same time. "Who wants to be the sower?" Alan asked, looking around the table. Kevin ended up playing a seed that fell into some weeds and got choked to death by Amy Peterson, a weed. They did this to show how sometimes the Word of God falls in places where it doesn't sink in for people because of the bad influence of others. Everyone laughed at the skits, and with the ice thus broken, Kevin was glad he came. As he later watched Eric's group perform their skit, Kevin had to laugh. Eric played a bridegroom with a bunch of girls playing bridesmaids coming out to greet him.

Figures, Kevin thought, *Eric always finds some way to get a bunch of girls around him.*

At lunch Eric ambled over to eat with Kevin. "Hey, that wasn't too bad," Eric said. "Not too religious, I mean." Eric shoved half a hot dog into his mouth. As he chewed, he mumbled, "Hey, what's bugging you?"

"Can you keep a secret?" asked Kevin.

"Sure. What's the problem?"

"*You* are."

"*Me*? Your best friend?"

"Eric, it bugs me that you're trying to pull a fast one with this service project while the rest of us are trying to take it seriously. It's not fair."

"What's not fair about it? It'll work, won't it?"

"I always thought you were strong," said Kevin as he looked down at the hot dog and potato chips on the paper plate in front of him.

"Of course I'm strong. I lift weights every day. I could have moved that table of yours all by myself!"

Kevin formed into words a thought that had come to him during the morning. "I don't think a man is strong if he doesn't live up to his word."

"What's that supposed to mean?" Eric asked.

"I mean if you're not strong enough to face your parents and say you don't want to be confirmed, then I'm not sure that I...."

"That you what?"

"That I want to have you as a friend." Kevin felt hot again and wondered if he should have kept his mouth shut.

"Hey, Kevin, let's not make somethin' out of nothin'. Who's going to help me with my homework?"

"That's the way I see it, Eric."

"Well, if that's the way you see it, you know where you can shove it!" said Eric, getting up. He propelled his plate at Kevin and sent potato chips flying all over the table, floor, and Kevin's lap. A few other kids temporarily noticed the ruckus but then went back to eating and talking. Kevin brushed the chips carefully off his lap and laid them in a pile beside his plate. He finished his lunch alone and was glad that no one else came to sit by him.

❄   ❄   ❄

After lunch Father Seroka told a few jokes while the team cleaned up, and the Confirmation candidates settled back into their groups. Kevin enjoyed the relief from not having to sit with Eric. He tried his best to put the whole problem out of his mind and pay attention to Father Seroka's talk.

"You know, a lot of people, not just kids, think that church is a drag — that God is a big policeman in the sky telling you what you shouldn't do. This morning you heard some ideas like that, I'll bet.

"And why do people say that? Because for them that's the way it is. They've heard that God is love, but they've never felt it. They've heard that church means community, but they haven't experienced it. They've heard about the Holy Spirit, but for them, it's just an invisible idea. What they're missing is what you felt a little of this morning. What they're missing is the reality of God's life in a way that they can experience it and recognize it, like you did in the skits and in your discussions. There are many names for living the Christian life — life in the Spirit, Christ-centered life, and so on. Those terms aren't something strange or abstract. They mean something *real*. A Spirit-filled life is something that happens whenever people care about one another, like the way your youth ministry team prepared this day for you. And it's something that happens whenever people forget about themselves and try to help one another, the way you helped one another when you put on your skits."

Kevin started to feel guilty. He wondered if he'd been too hard on Eric.

"When you kids were baptized," continued Father Seroka, "you were immersed in the life of God, which you found in your families

— a life of love and acceptance, care, and support. You received the life of Jesus from your parents, brothers, sisters, teachers, even coaches and scout leaders. Those are the people who have cared about you and helped you grow into the fine young people that you are today."

Some of the kids rolled their eyes or smiled.

"Sure, I see some of you smile at that," said Father Seroka. "I'll bet it wasn't always easy. You probably had fights at home, and other people probably gave you a rough time as well. Maybe there were times when life wasn't easy. Maybe your parents lost a job or got divorced. Maybe you had to deal with alcoholism or a death. Maybe you moved around so much that noplace ever felt like home, and it seemed hopeless to try to make friends. I know you've *all* lost friends; it happens to everybody. You've been on losing teams in sports, and you've all had those painful moments when you just wanted to crawl into a hole and die."

Kevin felt that way now. He wondered how Eric was feeling.

"But you didn't die," the priest went on. You made it through, somehow. And when you look back on your life, no matter how long or short it seems to you, you have to admit that you received a lot of goodness too. It came to you not because you were somebody great but just because you were you, and just because a lot of people have loved you. It came to you as a free gift or, as we sometimes say, as grace. Since all good things come from God, the goodness that you've received in your life thus far is all gift, it's all grace. It's grace that came through the love that people gave you. You received it, and you lived, and you grew.

"Jesus said we have received freely, now we should give freely. That means that at some time in your life you have to make a choice. You can live the rest of your life as a taker, or you can decide to be a giver. You can remain on the receiving end and stay a child forever, or you can make a conscious decision to live your life as a mature adult in the Church. And that means deciding to live the way Jesus did — giving love to other people and sharing God's life with them. That's why we have asked you to wait until you're older before being confirmed. If you were confirmed when you were a lot younger, you probably couldn't do more for other people than you already do in your own families, on your sports teams, or in the youth group. Some of you might help out in church on weekends, or do scout service projects, but that's about it.

"But now you're older. Now you're old enough to affirm the life of God in you and decide to share that life with others.

"People sometimes talk about 'receiving Confirmation,' but the truth is, in Confirmation you don't 'receive' anything. You have already received the Holy Spirit through Baptism, and you've been living the life of grace ever since you were a baby. What happens in Confirmation is a sign — a laying on of hands and an anointing that says 'We pray that the Spirit will be poured out on you even more in the future, to make your life richer, fuller and happier.' "

Kevin realized that he had tried to do that with Eric...and failed.

Father Seroka continued, "Love is the only thing that when you give it away, you have more of it. You have more of it in you because sometimes your heart has to grow to love people who don't seem very lovable. And you have more of it from others because the more love that you give away, the more love people give back to you.

"Our parish is named for the Blessed Trinity. The Trinity is a mystery. That's because love is a mystery. It's the most mysterious thing in human life, and that's because love is the life of God.

"In the Trinity, the Father loves the Son and the Son loves the Father. In turn, that giving and receiving of love within God generates a spiritual energy that is so much like God that it *is* God. And that's what we call the Holy Spirit. It's the Spirit that is generated in our own lives whenever we give and receive love.

"Now, I don't mean any kind of love. There are lots of things called love in our society that I'm not referring to. Many love songs, for example, are not about that special kind of love that we call the love of God. The love of God is the kind of love that accepts people just as they are — the way God accepts each one of us. It's the kind of love that reaches out to people and cares for them, even if they bite the hand that's trying to feed them.

"The first part of our program was devoted to helping you decide whether you really want to go through with Confirmation at this point in your lives. It was to help you decide whether you really want to make a personal commitment to sharing God's life with others."

Eric has to make his own decision, Kevin thought, *and live with the consequences.*

"We're here with you to help you get into the second part of our Confirmation program — the part that will begin with the sacrament and go on for at least a year after that. Hopefully, it will go on for a lifetime after that. To help you get started in the second part of the program, Mrs. Carter has invited some people from the parish to talk with you. They'll tell you what they do to share life with others in our community and how they've grown from doing that. There are many ways that you can grow through service to others, but today you only have to choose the one that seems the best to you right now."

There were people who worked one-on-one with the mentally disabled, the elderly, and with teenagers who had gotten themselves in trouble. Another group of adults served various organizations in the parish or the city like the St. Vincent de Paul Society, the scout programs for boys and girls, the soup kitchen, and the program to find housing for the homeless. There were also people who helped out with various religious education programs and political work for peace and social justice. All of the various groups needed volunteers to help them extend services to people they'd not been able to reach yet.

Then there were those who served the parish community. They were the ones Kevin usually saw and heard at weekend Masses lectoring or serving as Eucharistic ministers. They were also people who made things like banners to decorate the church and prepared parish meals like the Mother and Daughter Breakfast. When the general information sharing was over, Mrs. Carter stepped back in front of the group and said, "Each of you received a sheet on which you indicated your preferences for the type of help you'd like to give to people in need or to the life of the parish community. If you'll hand those in now, we'll sort them out and try to connect each of you with one of the service groups that you've just heard from.

"Your commitment to the service that selects you will be for one year. After that, you're on your own. But that's an adult responsibility, just as much as this one is. As an adult you have to make your own decisions all the time."

Kevin wondered what Eric was thinking when he heard this.

"We hope that a year from now you will decide to continue your work of service, or that you'll go on to another. But we trust that you'll all continue in your commitment to invite God's Spirit to keep growing within you by giving your love and devoting your talents to the service of others. That's the only way to keep growing in the life of God. Unfortunately, not everyone can have their first choices. Right now the team is trying to sort out your requests and match them with the needs that are out there. I'm sure you'll find, though, that no matter which work of service you find a place in, you'll find it to be rewarding work."

Mrs. Carter talked a while longer, and then Alan handed her a stack of all the papers.

"At the tables in the back you see the people you just heard," she said. "They'll welcome you into their service group and explain all you need to know in order to get started during the week after your Confirmation. As I read off your name, go to the table with the sign that has your service group's name on it."

She started calling off names: "Amy Peterson...you'll be tutoring children in math...."

Kevin listened as she called many names. His own was still not among them.

"Michael Marcovich...you'll help with the church decorating committee...."

A small group still sat scattered among the empty spaces in the front of the hall.

"The rest of you," Mrs. Carter went on, "are those who chose services that we don't have representatives for, or who did not indicate second and third preferences on your application forms.

"Kevin, you'll be in the tutorial program along with Amy Peterson and some others. Sadie, Eric, Jeff...if you'll come with me I'll let you know where help is needed in the parish so you can get placed in a service program before the day is out."

❋ ❋ ❋

Just before the closing liturgy that afternoon, Eric found his way back to Kevin and sat down next to him.

"You'll never guess what service program I signed up for," said Eric, smiling as though he'd just pulled a fast one.

Kevin looked at him suspiciously and said, "OK, so I give up. Tell me."

"I convinced them that I was smart enough to be a tutor too."

"Get off it!" said Kevin.

"No, really. I was thinking about what you said."

"Oh, yeah? Did you think about the little kids that you'll be disappointing too?"

"Hey, get off your high horse. I decided to go through with it."

Kevin wasn't sure if Eric was being honest with him or just pulling his leg.

Eric pleaded with him. "I'm telling you the truth, I swear. I thought about it all afternoon. You might be right. And besides that, you showed me how to get out of my problem."

"*I* showed you?"

"Sure. I figured it wouldn't be such a drag if you and me — well, if we could do something together. And maybe I could help with kids who hate school just as much as me."

Kevin still wasn't sure that Eric would stick to his commitment for a year. "Well, at least you'll have me to keep an eye on you."

"Not only that," Eric came back, "you'll have me to keep an eye on you and Amy!"

"Good grief," sighed Kevin, his romantic hopes dashed. "With friends like you, who needs warts?"

❊ ❊ ❊

"My, you look handsome in that suit," said Mrs. Whalen as she adjusted Kevin's tie.

"Mom, why didn't they ask us to pick Confirmation names?" The question had been on Kevin's mind for some time, though it came out only now on Confirmation day.

"Why do you ask?"

"Eric's dad says that when he was confirmed, everyone had to choose a saint's name for Confirmation."

"Kevin is a perfectly good saint's name. Didn't you hear at one of the evening meetings when Mr. Hanlon explained that? He said that those who really wanted to could choose a new name for Confirmation, but it's optional now in this diocese."

"I guess I wasn't listening," Kevin said.

"I did ask Mrs. Carter about it after the meeting, but she pointed out that in the early days of Christianity people didn't choose saints' names. They were expected to turn their own name into a saint's name. I like that."

"Aw, Mom, I'm too young to be a saint!"

"Maybe, but who knows? Maybe a hundred years from now there'll be a statue somewhere of Saint Kevin Whalen, patron saint of after-school tutors."

"I'd rather be the patron saint of scuba divers!"

"First things first. There'll be plenty of time for you to learn scuba diving if you want to, *after* you're confirmed."

"Uncle Charles says that I'm already pretty good at snorkeling."

"You're growing up fast, Kevin. I'm glad you asked him to be your Confirmation sponsor. He's seen you grow a lot these past two years."

"Is that why you suggested him?"

"That's one reason. The other reason is that your godparents live quite far from here. They don't know you as well as he does. A sponsor should be someone who can say, 'This person's ready to be confirmed in the Church.'"

"Amy asked Chuck Gillespie from the youth ministry to be her sponsor. I didn't know girls could ask men to be their sponsors. I thought only boys could have men for sponsors."

"No, anyone can be your sponsor, as long as the person's a practicing Catholic who isn't your parent. That's the main thing that matters. Why? Do you wish you had asked a woman to be your sponsor?"

"No, I was just wondering. I'm glad I picked Uncle Charles."

"I'm glad too. Now go see if your sister's ready."

❄   ❄   ❄

For the Confirmation ceremony each of the boys and girls had made a red stole to wear, showing the Holy Spirit on one side and something symbolizing their service work on the other. The teens joked among themselves about their homespun artistry to dispel the last-minute nervousness that rippled through the crowd.

"Hey, Kevin, you were supposed to make the Holy Spirit, not Daffy Duck!" The comment, of course, came from Eric.

"Yeah, well yours looks more like a bald eagle than a dove!" was Kevin's rejoinder.

"So, what of it? At least my bird's got some character, not like some of the wimpy pigeons I see around here!" said Eric.

The chatter died down quickly, though, when Bishop Knowles arrived and took his place at the rear of the processional line. The entrance song by the school choir gave the signal for everyone to begin walking slowly into church.

Some of the candidates looked as solemn as participants in a funeral. Others, like Eric, strutted in as though everything was cool. Kevin sensed all the eyes turned on them as they filed into the front pews. Parents, brothers, sisters, grandparents, teachers, and various people from the parish ministries filled the rest of the church.

Streamers and garlands of flowers festooned the altar and numerous candles glowed. The bishop praised the parish for the extraordinary support they had shown in making this a meaningful sacrament for everyone involved.

After the opening prayers and Scripture readings, Bishop Knowles returned to his praise of the parish as he addressed his sermon to the candidates. "I visit many parishes during the year, but coming to Blessed Trinity for Confirmation is always a treat for me. The Holy Spirit is present in every parish in our diocese, but this is one place where the Spirit's presence is truly *visible*. I can see it in the care you've taken to prepare today's liturgy. I can hear it in the way you sing. I can sense it in the warmth with which you greet one another when you meet. But the place that I especially see the Spirit's work is in your many parish ministries.

"At Confirmation time each year we often hear a good deal about the gifts of the Holy Spirit, but a gift is not much good unless you use it. It's clear to me that you are not only using the gifts God gave you, but you are developing them and growing as you use them in the service of others.

"We don't usually think about growing in giftedness. We can speak of someone as a gifted athlete or artist, but we would not say that about them if they had never developed their gift to the point where people noticed it. In your parish service programs many of you use the talents God has given you, and in doing that, you develop your gifts and enjoy the fruits of using them.

"When we speak about the gifts of the Holy Spirit, though, we mean more than natural talents, which in their own way are gifts from God. We talk about the gifts of faith, hope, and love; the gifts of knowledge and wisdom; the gifts of judgment and courage; the gifts of wonder and reverence. These are what might be called spiritual gifts, as opposed to natural gifts, yet they are all talents that need to be developed if we are going to experience the fullness of them and if others are going to appreciate them in us.

"We can think about the gift of faith as trusting in God's call to do good to others even when they don't appreciate it. We can think about Christian hope as that vision of all the good that will come from doing good for others as Jesus did. We can think about love as that force found in Jesus' way of giving, which asked for nothing in return.

"*Knowledge* is the gift of thinking clearly and seeing the world as it is. *Wisdom* is the ability to see how what we are doing fits into the bigger picture of God's plan for human happiness. *Understanding* means 'heart-knowledge,' knowing the feelings and the attitudes of another's heart. *Judgment* is that knack for making good decisions when we are faced with a number of options. *Courage* is the endurance that helps us see our decisions through to the end. *Wonder* is the ability to look at the world with the amazement of a child. *Reverence* means being serious in a very adult way — always treating others with respect. At least that's one way of thinking about these gifts.

"But there are other spiritual gifts too, such as being fair, open, and honest with people — putting their needs ahead of our own and being happy with their success even when our own wishes may not be granted. The ability to pray and hear God speaking to you when you pray or read the Scriptures are gifts that are important for every adult Christian. The ability to keep going when the chips are down, not worrying about tomorrow but being thankful for all the good that God gives today…these are all gifts of the very highest order. Yet even these are not all of them.

"My point is not to list or explain all God's gifts, but to help you realize how gifted each of you already are. You were gifted with your natural talents just by being born. You were further gifted by the families that you grew up in. More gifts came to you through your Baptism when you became a member of the Church and its community.

"Today we pray that you will receive the Holy Spirit. But how can you receive this gift if it's already been given to you in Baptism? The answer is simple but often overlooked. Jesus gave us the answer in his parable of the servants whose master gave them money but only two of them used the gifts he gave them. The third one got the money but then he did nothing with it. He did not accept it as something to do good with. Instead he did nothing with it, which is why the master called him lazy and ungrateful. Because he did not use it, he did not really receive the gift that had been given to him.

"Our celebration this evening is called Confirmation. In it, the Church confirms the fact that you have been given the Holy Spirit and many other spiritual gifts. In a little while I will anoint your forehead and say to each of you, 'Be sealed with the gift of the Holy Spirit.' When an envelope is sealed, it already has something inside it. When a document has an official seal on it, everything in that document becomes official. So what I'm asking you to do when I anoint you is to be like that envelope and like that document. We are asking you to show that you have God's Spirit within you. That's a tough job. It's a job that takes a lifetime. That's why you are confirmed just once, just as you are baptized only once. But it gives your life a certain character. It affects your personality, making you more like Christ in a way that others can see.

"When people looked at Jesus they saw that God's Spirit was in him. That's why they called him the Christ, the Messiah, the Anointed One. And that's why you too will be anointed, as a symbol of God's Spirit dwelling in you. It's not easy to be like Christ. Fortunately, though, it's not a job we have to do alone. The Spirit helps us from within, and the Church helps us with support, encouragement, and opportunities to grow in Christ. Before you are anointed, therefore, the Church asks that you remember the commitment that was made on your behalf by your godparents. Now is the time for you to confirm that commitment in your own words by standing on your own behalf and renewing your baptismal promises."

After the baptismal promises, the candidates remained standing while Bishop Knowles addressed the congregation, reading from the sacramentary: "My dear friends, in Baptism God gave us the new birth of eternal life to be among a chosen people. Let us pray that the Holy Spirit will strengthen these sons and daughters with grace-filled gifts and help them to be more like Christ the Son of God."

All prayed silently for a while, after which the bishop and the priests extended their hands in blessing over the candidates. Then, one by one, the candidates approached the bishop with their sponsors.

As he took each step closer toward the altar, Kevin heard the bishop's voice more clearly until he could make out every word.

When his turn came, Kevin felt his uncle's hand on his shoulder while the bishop anointed his forehead with the sign of the cross and said, "Kevin, be sealed with the gift of the Holy Spirit."

"Amen," responded Kevin.

"Peace be with you," affirmed the bishop, looking right into Kevin's eyes.

"And also with you," answered Kevin.

As Kevin walked back to his seat with Uncle Charles, he wondered whether something special or spiritual had really happened. It seemed less dramatic than what had happened the week before with Eric. He looked at Eric now, who seemed to be taking it all in as if the whole ceremony were just for him. Had Eric *really* changed inside or was he the same wheeler-dealer he'd always been?

Kevin glanced at Uncle Charles and then did a double take. *Wow! Uncle Charles is short!* he thought. It had been about four or five months since he'd last seen his uncle. *Has he shrunk or have I grown?* Kevin asked himself. He looked at Uncle Charles carefully so it wouldn't look like he was staring. When Kevin definitely realized what had happened, he smiled proudly and looked over at Eric. *Yep. I've grown all right!*

One Body; So Many Members!

(Holy Eucharist)

MEMORANDUM

FROM: *Father John Rodriguez*
TO: *Liturgical Commission*
SUBJECT: *First Communion Liturgy*

Sorry I can't be with you at your next meeting, but I know you'll do a terrific job even in my absence. You have grown a great deal in your understanding of liturgy and worship during the time that we have been working together. The Holy Week services and the liturgies of the Easter Vigil and Easter Sunday were the most beautiful that I have ever experienced in our parish. Keep up the good work!

Apart from the regular Saturday/Sunday Masses, the only liturgies that we need to devote particular attention to in the coming months are those of Ascension Thursday and Pentecost. You may also want to think about doing something special for Mother's Day. This year, however, I would also like to do something a little different for our First Communion celebration, which will be the third Sunday in May.

In the past, the emphasis seems to have been on individual devotion to Jesus in the receiving of Communion. This year I would like to try to put more of the focus on the community dimension of the Eucharistic meal.

How we go about doing that, I am not exactly sure yet. But you have done so well in the past that I feel confident I can turn it over to you and trust that your creativity will come up with something wonderful for the whole parish.

I have also sent a memo with a similar request to Mrs. Fallon, our director of religious education, asking that she try to orient this spring's First Communion preparation program in the same direction. I shall be keeping in contact with her and with you during the next few weeks to see how things are going, but it might also be good if some of your commission members get together with Mrs. Fallon to share ideas and coordinate your efforts. Please feel free to call on me anytime for advice or assistance.

❇   ❇   ❇

"Well, what do you think?" asked Roger.

Lillian was the first to respond. "I had been sort of hoping that things would get a little more relaxed around here now that we've gotten past Easter! But I can see why Father Rodriguez wants us to devote so much time to liturgy planning. The Mass is the main chance most people have to learn about their faith each week, as well as to celebrate it."

Hernando was a little more enthusiastic. "I really like the idea of doing something new for First Communion. My twins will both be preparing for it this year."

Across the dining room table in the rectory, Renee sat pensively, then offered, "It's going to be a real challenge. Like Father said, many people have the idea that Communion is just a Jesus-and-me sacrament. We've tried to bring in the *community* aspect of Communion to our liturgies, but we've never coordinated our efforts with the sacrament preparation program before. Still, if Father John thinks we can do it, it's worth a try!"

Roger asked, "Renee, would you be willing to be our contact person with Mrs. Fallon and the people who are putting together the First Communion preparation program? Then, when we get together next week, we'll have a better idea of where they are and where we ought to be going with this."

"I'd be happy to do it and get out of the house some nights after all these years. But don't tell my husband that!"

"Fine, it's settled then," said Roger. "We'll keep your secret! Now let's start planning the liturgies for next weekend."

❄ ❄ ❄

"I don't like it one bit!" Hernando's wife was adamant.

"But Juanita," her husband insisted, "the pastor says that we should do it this way. How can you argue with the pastor?"

"Pastor?" Juanita said. "It's that Mrs. Fallon with her new ideas! Who ever heard of such things? Did you see the letter she sent home with Teresa and Carlos?"

"Yes, but...."

"Yes, but nothing. Last year it was no going to confession before First Communion. Now this year she wants us to give up white dresses and veils for the girls and white suits for the boys! Who is she to tell us what to do?"

"Mrs. Fallon doesn't make those decisions by herself, Juanita. Father John and the religious education board have to approve everything."

"Does the pope know about this? I heard that Rome wanted children to make their first confession before going to Communion. I know. Monsignor Salvi told me."

"The Italian connection," said Hernando, rolling his eyes toward the heavens. "Look, Monsignor Salvi has his way of looking at it, and he tells you what you want to hear. Did he tell you that bishops can make adjustments for the pastoral needs of their own dioceses?"

"Adjustments, nothing. They didn't make any 'adjustments' in the monsignor's parish. Throwing it out is what I call it. Who ever heard of not going to confession before Communion?"

"Plenty of people. You see all the people who go to Communion now on Sundays. But when you go to confession every Saturday, how many people do you see?" Hernando asked.

"Why don't *you* come sometime and see for *yourself?* It's not like the old days. People don't know right from wrong anymore. I don't think they've taught our children about mortal and venial sin. How do they expect children to be good if they don't tell them what sins they shouldn't commit?"

"There's plenty of time for that when the children are older," her husband countered. "You don't have to fill their heads with grown-up ideas when they're only seven. Studies have shown that kids are psychologically not ready for it then."

"Psychology?" Juanita charged, "If it was psychology, why don't they let the children wear white? Don't they know that children *like* to dress up? It makes them feel special. It tells them that Communion is important — and different from just going to church."

"I think our children know that. Carlos and Teresa have been asking to go to Communion ever since they were five. But they should still understand something about it first."

"Aha! Now *you're* the one who's saying they should understand first! A minute ago you were saying they don't need to understand."

"That was about sin and threats of punishment and all that business. This is about the meaning of Communion."

"The meaning of Communion is that it is the body and blood of Christ. And when you receive it, Jesus comes into your soul in a way that you can *feel*. That's why children should dress up, to get ready to meet Jesus!"

"Juanita, there's much more to Communion than that. The theology of the Eucharist…well, there's more to it now."

"Theology? What do *you* know about theology? All you know is what you hear at those silly meetings you go to every week."

"Really, Juanita, you ought to get more involved in the life of the parish. Then you'd understand."

"Get more involved, he says! Whatever happened to the good old days when *involved* meant being an usher or helping to clean the church? But no, I have to marry a man who goes to meetings all the time and then tells me that the Church is different!"

"At least you're coming to the parents' meeting tomorrow night, no?"

"But only to see why they're turning everything upside down!"

❉ ❉ ❉

"Good evening, ladies and gentlemen. *Buenas tardes, señores y señoras.* For those of you who have not met me yet, my name is Joyce Fallon. I don't get to meet as many of you as my coworkers do because they work more closely with the people in the parish, whereas I spend most of my time as director of religious education and working closely with the teachers.

"Our First Communion preparation program this year is really going to be a parishwide experience, involving not only the children and their families but many of our teachers, the liturgical commission, and the youth choir. We want *everyone* in the parish — not only you and your families — to know what an important event First Communion will be for your children.

"Father Rodriguez, of course, has had a lot to do with this. He has given us a great deal of inspiration and leadership, but he has also given us the freedom to be creative in developing the very best approach for our bilingual parish. I would, therefore, like to begin the program this evening with a few words from our pastor."

"*Gracias*, Mrs. Fallon," said Father Rodriguez as he clutched the sides of the lectern. "It's so good to see so many of you here tonight. You are all parents whose children are finishing second grade. Your sons and daughters have reached what has been traditionally called the 'age of reason.' Not that kids are always reasonable, far from it!" Laughter rippled through the crowd. "But they can understand things when we give them reasons for them starting somewhere around the age of seven. And understanding the Eucharist is something that takes a little explaining. Our children need it, and we need it too, for we never fully comprehend the mystery of the Eucharist.

"It is because we always need to keep growing in our appreciation of the Eucharist that our First Communion preparation program has grown so much. For some time now, we have had evening sessions such as this one for parents such as yourselves. Parents are the primary religious educators of their children — whether they want to be or not! You teach your children every day about the meaning and importance of religion in your lives. And so it is necessary that you grow in your understanding of religion, not only for your own sake but also for theirs.

"Last year in our parish we took that idea and put it into practice by introducing a home-instruction program for parents to teach their own children. This helps families learn to live a happier, more Christian life together. We also developed some lessons for parents to teach their children who were preparing for First Communion. You'll hear more about that later this evening, I'm sure, if you haven't already heard about it from your friends.

"This year I have asked the people on the parish liturgical commission to help plan the liturgy at which your children will make their First Communion. The youth choir will also be helping with the music, which will make our celebration on that day a lively and memorable one for all of us, I'm sure. And on two Sundays before the children make their First Communion, everyone in the parish will be treated to special sermons from a guest preacher, Deacon Snyder, who will speak about the community dimension of the Eucharistic liturgy.

"This year, though, we already have many things planned to make First Communion a wonderful experience for your children, for yourselves, and for everyone in the parish. Since Mrs. Fallon and I are the coordinators for sacrament preparation in our parish, we have already sent you a letter outlining our program for this year. Did all of you receive it? Are there any questions you'd like to ask Mrs. Fallon or me?"

Juanita's hand shot up. "Why don't the children have to make their first confession anymore before being allowed to go to Communion?"

"That's a good question," replied the coordinator. "In fact, it's so good that our speaker next week will give it special treatment. I'd like to wait until then to talk about it so as not to repeat what he says. Are there any other questions?"

"Yes," said Juanita before anyone else could answer. Hernando slumped a little lower in his chair. "What's this business about the children not dressing up for their First Communion this year? I think that deprives them of something they will always remember."

"Hmm, I don't remember writing anything about the children not dressing up," said Mrs. Fallon. "What I did say was that parents did not have to buy white First Communion outfits especially for the occasion. If they want to do that, it's fine, but I know that buying new clothes might be a hardship for some families, so Father John and I decided that white clothes would be optional. Also, on that day the children will be seated with their families so they can make their First Communion with their older brothers and sisters, their mother and their father. Since they won't be seated as a group, there's no need for them to dress uniformly."

"And what about the kids whose parents don't go to Communion or don't even go to church regularly?" insisted Juanita. "Are you going to deprive those children of Holy Communion?"

"That sounds like a policy question to me," said Mrs. Fallon. "Father John, would you care to answer that?"

"Surely." The pastor stepped back up to the lectern. "Mrs. Fallon, the teachers, and I felt very strongly that if a child's parents don't go to church, he or she probably won't be going to church much, either. And the same holds true, more or less, for children whose parents don't go to Communion, for whatever reason. It relates to what I said before about parents teaching more by example than we ever can with words, even if the children go to our parochial school.

"Eucharist is a sacrament of initiation. You'll hear more about that in the coming weeks, I'm sure, and I think you would agree that a child's First Communion should be just that. It should certainly not be his or her last Communion! It should be the beginning of a deeper relationship with Jesus and of a greater involvement with the life of the Church.

"Of course, every now and then there are children whose parents are not religious but who have other relatives or friends in the parish who take them to church. Those relatives and friends are here tonight, and they'll see to it that the child's First Communion experience is a good one. We really do try to go out of our way to reach every child who wants to grow in their faith.

"Then, too, seven is not a magic age for making First Communion. Some parents don't think their children are ready for it yet, and they decide to wait a year or two. By having the kids sit with their families and not lumping them in a group, we feel we're taking some of the pressure off to make First Communion just because everybody else in the second grade is.

"So if Catholic children without religious parents want to make their First Communion when they're nine or eleven or thirteen, they can do that too. All they need is someone who will be family for them in the parish. A number of our Catholic school teachers have already done that for kids in their classes."

"That's certainly very different from when I was a child," commented Juanita. Her voice was still insistent.

"Yes, it is. Children's needs today are often different from what they were twenty or thirty years ago. And in that time the Church has also grown in its understanding of the Eucharist. We are always adapting and growing. But your question was a good one."

"Thanks again, Father," said Mrs. Fallon, returning to her place at the lectern. "Are there any other questions, then, about the information in the letter you received?"

The remaining questions were mostly practical, dealing with the schedule of events or what if someone couldn't make it to one of the evening sessions, or how to use the teaching materials that were going to be provided, and the like. But none of the questions were as dramatic as Juanita's — perhaps because none of the questioners felt as passionately as she did about her beliefs.

On their way out of the school hall, Hernando turned to Juanita. "Did you hear that? They both said you asked good questions."

"Good questions, nothing. What I want are some good answers. I don't know that I buy what Father Rodriguez said. And did you see what that other one did? She just put me off!"

"She just wanted you to come and hear a better answer next week," said Hernando, hoping that one day she would understand.

❄   ❄   ❄

"What? No liturgy commission meeting tonight?" asked Juanita, with a touch of sarcasm in her voice.

Hernando was sunk in the overstuffed sofa, an open Bible on his lap. "I'm doing homework instead."

"What sort of homework?" his wife asked, walking into the living room while drying her hands with the dishtowel.

"I'm supposed to pick the readings for the First Communion Mass. One from the Gospels and one from some other part of the Bible," explained Hernando.

"Since when did they start letting ordinary people pick the readings?"

Hernando could not resist. "Since the Second Vatican Council — about twenty years ago."

"Is that so? Oh, wait, I remember now how we helped select the readings for our wedding. But how did *you* get the job?"

"Because I'm on the liturgical commission. And because I have two children who will be making their First Communion that day."

"*I* have two children too!" his wife reminded him. "Why couldn't *I* pick them out?"

"I have a better idea, *cara*. Why don't you call the *niños* and we'll let them help us."

"Teresa! Carlos! Your father wants to see you in the living room! Right away!"

The two little ones raced in and bounced onto the sofa, one on either side of their father.

"What's up? What do you want us for?" the children asked.

"I want you to help me."

"With what, Papa?"

"You know that soon you'll be making your First Communion."

"Uh-huh."

"And when we go to Mass we always hear some stories from the Bible."

"Uh-huh. Only I don't always like them."

"Really, Teresa? Why not?"

"Because I don't always understand them."

"I'm glad you said that because my job is to pick some stories for your First Communion Mass. Which Bible stories do you like?"

"I like the one about David and Goliath," said Carlos right away.

"And I like the one about Judith, who chopped the bad king's head off!" announced Teresa.

"Hmm. I'm glad to see that you remember the stories that your mama reads to you at bedtime. But we need some different stories."

"What kind?"

"Some stories about Jesus. Which stories about Jesus do you remember?"

"I like the part where he was born in a stable, and a star came out, and three kings came," offered Teresa.

"And there's the part at the end, where the bad guys kill him on the Cross. They wouldn't have done that if I was there. I would have called G.I. Joe and his commandos to come and rescue him!" Carlos raised an imaginary rifle to his shoulder and started firing in all directions.

"Carlos!" his shocked mother said.

"Well, uh," Hernando went on. "I can see we're getting closer. How about something in between?"

"In between what?"

"In between the birth of Jesus and his death. Like some stories about when he was grown up."

"I like the way he made all the sick people well," said Teresa.

"Yeah. Or like the time he found a guy all beaten up by robbers,

63

and he took him to a hotel and patched him up," said Carlos, giving his best effort.

His mother could not resist correcting him. "That's a story Jesus *told*. It's not something that he *did*."

"I like it anyway," said the boy in self-defense.

Hernando decided that maybe he should try a more direct approach. "How about the story of Jesus' Last Supper with his disciples? Do you know that one?"

"Sure," said Carlos. "We have a picture of it in our dining room."

"Good! That's one we can use." Hernando breathed a sigh of relief. "We're making progress."

"And you know which one I like?" said Teresa. "It's the time when the disciples tried to chase all the children away. But Jesus said it's OK if they sit on his lap. I even heard that one at church...I think."

"I did too! Father John told it," Carlos remembered.

"Well, what do you think?" Hernando asked, looking at his wife.

"They're two nice stories, but they're both from the Gospel. You can't have two Gospels at Mass."

"I think I know a way to avoid that problem. Children, you've been very helpful. Now give your papa a kiss and off to bed!"

❄   ❄   ❄

"As Mrs. Fallon just explained," began Deacon Donald Snyder as he shifted through his notes at the lectern, "the purpose of these evening sessions in the First Communion preparation program is not so much to tell you what to teach your children but to help you adults grow in your own knowledge and appreciation of the Eucharist. The religious education staff here at St. James' believes that if you have a mature understanding of this sacrament, you'll be able to participate more fully in the Mass every week. You'll be able to talk with more assurance about the Eucharist. That way you'll be able to answer your children's questions better, not only before they make their First Communion but also as they're growing up. And I'm happy to say that I agree with that approach.

"I'll be with you for two meetings and, as you know already, I will also be preaching at the Sunday Masses for the next two weeks, sharing some insights and reflections on the Eucharist with you and the other members of the parish. So I won't try to cover everything tonight!

"What I'd like to do, then, is use this evening to review with you the origin and history of the Eucharistic liturgy, or the Mass as we call it. I'll bring out some important theological ideas and practical implications. Since this week will be rather heavy with just my lecture, next week will be devoted mainly to discussion. I hope that's all right with you."

"I thought that woman said my 'good question' would be answered *this* week!" Juanita whispered to her husband.

"Shh. Maybe it will be," said Hernando.

"The first thing that I would like to present to you this evening is a brief but interesting video on the history of the Mass. It's called *Worshipping Wilma,* and it's produced by Franciscan Communications in Los Angeles. It shows how the Eucharist began with Jesus' Last Supper and the apostles before he died. It also shows how the practice of sharing bread and wine continued and evolved in the Christian community over many centuries. Now it's the Mass that we have in the Church today.

"I would especially like you to pay attention to two facts as you view this presentation. The first is that Eucharistic worship in the Church did, in fact, *evolve* and *change* during the past twenty centuries. The basic aspects of the liturgy always remained the same, though. The second is that Eucharistic theology has also changed through the centuries, reflecting the changes in people's experience of worship, although some aspects of this have likewise remained the same. It's important to see this in order to understand the difference between the unchanging essence of the Eucharist and the changeable appearance of the Eucharist in many different centuries and cultures."

Deacon Snyder turned out the lights and flipped on the monitor.

A few minutes into the presentation, Juanita nudged her husband and whispered, "I don't think I like the way this show makes something that is *serious* into something that looks like a *cartoon*!"

Hernando said nothing.

When the lights came back on, Deacon Snyder turned to the audience and said, "Let's see now how much you have learned. I asked you to look for some things as you viewed the video. First, which things in Eucharistic worship *remained the same* down through the centuries?"

As the parents responded, he wrote their correct responses on the sheet for the overhead projector:

(1) Gathering the community together for worship
(2) Presided over by bishop or priest
(3) Readings from the Scriptures
(4) Offering gifts of bread and wine
(5) Prayers of praise, thanksgiving, and petition
(6) Memorial of Jesus' Last Supper
(7) Sharing of Communion.

"Very good," he said, commenting on the group's attentiveness. "Now I'll try to summarize how the Mass has *changed* down through the centuries."

Taking out a clean transparency for the projector, he wrote on the screen for all to see:

(1) A.D. 30-300: Gathering in people's homes. More informal, like a meal.

(2) 300-600: Meeting in public basilicas. Much ceremony and participation.

(3) 600-1200: Building of large cathedrals. Greater distance between priest and people.

(4) 1200-1600: More loss of participation. Priest sometimes says Mass without people.

(5) 1600-circa 1965: Latin Mass with some local variations in all parts of the Catholic world.

(6) Circa 1965-present: Liturgy in a variety of styles, in different circumstances and cultures.

"You can see from this summary," Deacon Snyder continued, "that when the Second Vatican Council met in the 1960s, it encouraged changes in the liturgy. This was not something terribly new — even though it *seemed* new because the Mass had not changed much since 1600. In fact, the Council wanted the Church to *recover* some of the good things from the earlier centuries, which had gotten overlooked in the later centuries.

"First, gathering around a table, as it was in the beginning. This is why the altar was moved away from the back wall and made to look more like a table again.

"Second, worship in the language of the people. At one time *everyone* spoke Latin, so everyone could *understand* the Mass. But during the Middle Ages, Latin fell into disuse among the laity. As a result, the only people who understood the Mass' words, then, were clergy and religious.

"Third, participation in the liturgy. Not just the priest at the altar, but many ministers serving, reading, and leading the prayer responses. Also, more singing by the congregation.

"Fourth, variety in the liturgy. Now the Mass can be celebrated more informally again (in homes, for example), and it can also be adapted to meet people's need to worship in ways that they feel at home with.

"Very often, people can feel comfortable with the recent changes in the Mass once they understand the history of the changing Mass. But sometimes they are not so comfortable with the 'new' theology of the Eucharist. Let us see now whether this 'new' theology is really so new."

Once again the speaker encouraged the audience to recall what they had learned from the video about the essential aspects of Eucharistic theology, while he summarized the results for them on the overhead projector:

(1) Jesus established the Eucharist;
(2) Jesus is present in the Eucharist;
(3) Eucharistic worship is a form of sacrifice.

"Excellent," commented Deacon Snyder. "I can see you're really on the ball tonight. Now, let's see how many *developments* in the Church's understanding of the Eucharist have occurred."

Putting a new transparency on the projector, he wrote:

(1) A.D. 30-300: Emphasis on Jesus' presence in the worshiping community. Christians unite themselves with Christ's sacrifice to God.

(2) 300-600: Focus on Jesus' presence in the bread and wine. Worshipers share in priest's offering of Christ to God.

(3) 600-1200: Attention to change of bread and wine into body and blood of Christ. People watch priest offer sacrifice of Christ to the Father.

(4) 1200-1600: Change of bread and wine into body and blood of Christ explained by theory of *transubstantiation.*

(5) 1600-1970: Connection between priest's action at the altar and Christ's sacrifice on the Cross explained by theory of *participation.*

(6) 1970-present: Restoration of balance between earlier and later views about presence and sacrifice. Also, introduction of more modern theories about what happens during Eucharistic worship.

"Once again I must really congratulate you on your grasp of these basics," Deacon Snyder told the people. "To explain them fully would take an entire course in history and theology! But don't worry: I'm not going to try to do it all here tonight. Instead, I'd just like to point out a few things, as I did earlier.

"First, the Catholic Church has always believed in the presence of Christ in the Eucharist. This faith is based on Jesus' words over the bread and wine at the Last Supper. He said, 'Take and eat; this is my body.' Then he gave them the cup and said, 'Drink from it....for this is my blood.....' But it is also based on Christians' experience of Christ's presence in the Eucharist down through the centuries.

"Second, the word, 'Eucharist,' can be used to refer to the activity of liturgical worship. It can also be used to refer to the consecrated bread and wine. Thus, in the Church's history, sometimes the presence of Christ in the Eucharist has been emphasized in the liturgy, and sometimes the emphasis has been on the presence of Christ in the consecrated bread and wine.

"Third, when the emphasis is only on the sacramental bread and wine, people tend to forget that Christ is also present in the activity of liturgical worship. And when people forget Christ's presence in themselves as they worship, they often feel sinful compared to the holiness of the sacrament. When this happened in the early Middle Ages, many people stopped going to Communion because they felt unworthy to approach Christ in the sacrament. When this happened in modern times, between 1600 and 1970, people felt they had to have their sins forgiven in the sacrament of Reconciliation before they could receive Christ in Communion.

"Fourth, at the beginning of this century, Pope Pius X encouraged Catholics to receive Communion more frequently. However, since people had gotten used to the idea of always going to confession before going to Communion, they began to go to confession more frequently too. This pope also urged parents to let their children receive First Communion as soon as they had reached the so-called 'age of reason.' This age has been defined as the time when a child can understand that Christ is present in the Blessed Sacrament. However, this also led to the practice of making seven-year-olds go to confession before they could make their First Communion.

"Fifth, in recent decades, with the help of scriptural and historical scholarship, we have come to realize that we should not neglect Christ's presence among us in liturgical worship. We have also come to see that the practice of going to confession before Communion is a fairly late development in the Church's history. In the years since the Second Vatican Council, therefore, the Church has developed a more balanced view toward Christ's presence in the Eucharist. We now emphasize *both* his presence in the worshiping community *and* his presence in the Blessed Sacrament.

"Many Catholics understandably have moved away from the practice of always going to confession before Communion, since they no longer feel unworthy to approach Christ in the sacrament. And for this reason, too, many parishes have moved away from having children make their first confession before making their First Communion, even though some still prefer this approach."

"Was that the answer you were looking for?" asked Hernando, leaning toward his wife.

"That's the answer to my question," said Juanita, "but it is *not* the one that I was hoping for. Why couldn't things be simpler? This is so complicated. Things were much easier when I was young."

"Our time together for this evening is about over," said Deacon Snyder in conclusion. "This historical and theological material that we covered is somewhat complex, but you've been a very patient and appreciative audience. I am sure that you have questions about a number of the things I spoke about. Perhaps there are some things I didn't mention too. Please bring those questions with you when we meet next week.

"Before we leave tonight, however, I would like to leave you with one thought. Some people wonder why today we seem to have so much freedom in the Church — especially freedom to change from the way things were when we were younger. I find the answer to that puzzle in the facts of history and the words of Jesus. The facts of history show us that the liturgy and theology of the Eucharist have already undergone some truly marvelous changes. And the words of Jesus tell us, 'You will know the truth, and the truth will set you free.' "

❋   ❋   ❋

"Wow! Did you catch Deacon Snyder's lecture last week?" asked Renee as she walked into the rectory dining room.

"Pretty heady stuff, if you ask me," said Roger, who had already settled into his seat at the head of the table.

"I'll say," confirmed Lillian. "Once he got started, he didn't stop!"

"And he also…dropped a few bombs," added Hernando, after finding the right metaphor. "One of them he dropped right into the lap of my wife!"

"Don't tell me which one," joked Father Rodriguez. "I'll guess!"

"It was a good learning experience for all of us," commented Roger. "Which reminds me — did we all do our homework last week?"

After being assured that they all had brought something to contribute to the First Communion liturgy, the chairman continued. "Good. Now let's get down to the business of planning the liturgy for this coming weekend. Then we can take our coffee break, and after that we'll talk about what we've found out."

The group did not wait until after the break, however, to start sharing what they had learned. Already in the kitchen they were relating their experiences of the previous week.

"No wonder the first part of our meeting went so fast!" said the pastor, pouring the coffee. "You were all so eager to get to the second part!"

Hernando recounted his dialogue with his children on the couch, and Juanita judging their orthodoxy with a wave of the dishtowel. They could appreciate the humor of the scene, knowing his wife's strict approach and his children's playfulness.

"But what about the problem of the readings?" asked Lillian.

"No problem!" answered Hernando with a smile. "I knew all along that we could use Saint Paul's account of the Last Supper from his First Letter to the Corinthians for the first reading. So all I needed was a good Gospel story for the second reading. Father John, do you think we could use the one that my *niños* suggested — the one with Jesus and the children?"

"Perfect! Roger, did you think of a place in the liturgy where the children could come up and join me at the altar?"

"Well, Father, I like what you sometimes do at the Masses for children, letting them come up and sit around you for the homily. But last year at another parish I saw an idea that I also liked. At that

Mass the priest invited the children to come and stand around the altar during the Liturgy of the Eucharist."

"An excellent idea! Unfortunately, we priests don't have the luxury of seeing what other priests do on weekends. We're always so busy doing our own thing!"

"I thought it would go well," Roger continued, "with the fact that since this is their First Communion, they would all be 'gathered around the table of the Lord,' so to speak."

"And the kids are so little," Hernando pointed out, "that they are hardly able to see you from the pews, Father. This way they'll all feel much closer to you — and to Jesus and one another too."

"But the homily, then. What should we do for it?" inquired the pastor.

"The *words,* of course, we leave to you, Father! That's your department. But as for the way to do it," Roger went on, "I thought it would be good if we asked all of the First Communion families to sit close to the front, on both sides of the center aisle...."

"We could mark the area with a ribbon," interjected Lillian.

"...and then you could go down from the sanctuary to be closer to them. Maybe even a dialogue homily, talking with the children while explaining the readings."

"Sure. I've done that before. Say, is anyone writing all these ideas down?"

"Don't worry, Father! We won't forget them!" said Lillian.

"But I haven't told you *my* idea yet," said Renee, eagerly joining the circle around the coffee pot.

"We're all ears," said Roger. "What is it?"

"Mariachis!" announced Renee.

"Mariachis?" exclaimed several at once.

"Sure. The ones who played for the fiesta of Our Lady of Guadalupe. Sometimes people also pay them to play the mariachi Mass at big weddings," explained Renee.

"But they're expensive! How will we ever afford it?" asked Roger. "The liturgical commission doesn't have that kind of budget!"

"No need to afford it," said Renee. "I was talking with Andy, the youth minister, about the music for the Mass, and he said that guitar player, Pablo Sanchez, has a daughter who will be making her First Communion this year."

"I didn't realize that he was Maria Sanchez's father! I never see him at Mass," said the pastor with a frown.

"But her mother brings all her children to church every week," noted Lillian.

"Well, anyway, Andy talked Mr. Sanchez into getting his whole band to play for his daughter's First Communion!"

"The Mexican connection!" shouted Hernando.

"Wait a minute. Wait a minute. Andy can't make decisions like that on his own," insisted Father Rodriguez. "That's the job of the liturgical commission. What do all of you think about it?"

Looking around the group, Roger said, "It looks like we have consensus."

"Hmm, yes. But you still need one more thing," said Father Rodriguez, looking serious. "The approval of the pastor."

For a moment, no sound was heard except the traffic out in the street.

"And you have it!" said Father Rodriguez, smiling.

"You had me worried there for a second, Father," sighed Renee.

"Me too!" added Hernando.

"The only one who has to worry is Mr. Sanchez," said the pastor, looking serious again. "I'm going to pay him a little visit — about coming to church more often!"

❄ ❄ ❄

"Mama, look what I got!" shouted Carlos outside the church doors as he waited for his parents walking across the parking lot.

"I got one too," Teresa chimed in. "Pin it on me, Mama!"

"Where did you get this?" asked Juanita, fingering the enamel and gold pin of a chalice and host.

"Mrs. Fallon gave them to us. She had one for all the kids at the church door."

"Well," said Hernando knowingly, "now they all do have something special to wear, after all."

"It's very lovely," remarked Juanita, pinning it on Teresa's dress. "It reminds me of the one that I received on my own First Communion day," she said to Carlos as she pinned one on his shirt.

"Hurry up!" insisted Hernando. "I hear the music playing. We don't want to be the last ones in the church!"

Taking their children's hands, Juanita and Hernando dashed up the stairs into the vestibule.

"No need to rush," said the colorfully dressed pastor as he waited for the entrance procession to begin. "The mariachi band is just warming up."

"*Mariachis*? You didn't tell me about that," Juanita said, looking in her husband's direction.

"I said it was going to be a nice Mass, didn't I?" said Hernando with a twinkle.

"But look at all those people! *Madre de Dios!* Where did they all come from?"

"Just people in the parish who wanted to join in our celebration for our children." Hernando was trying to sound matter-of-fact, but he was not doing too well at concealing his delight. "Come, let's find some seats near the altar."

"Oh, the flowers and the banners. They're lovely," Juanita said, slowly drinking in the colorful sights and happy sounds.

Just as they found an empty pew, the music stopped. Then it began again, with the choir leading the entrance hymn. Carlos and Teresa, like most of the children, stood on tiptoes to catch a glimpse of the entrance procession.

"Well, Juanita, what do you think? Is it a nice First Communion Mass?" Hernando noticed that his wife was looking in her purse. When she found what she wanted, he saw it was a handkerchief.

"Oh my…" she said, taking his arm, "it's *beautiful!*"

It's Hard
to Turn Around

(Reconciliation/Penance)

The union strikers paced up and down the sidewalk in front of Demarist Manufacturing. It was the third week of the walkout. J. Quincy Demarist peeked through the blinds to watch the strikers from inside his office. A day of snow had thinned their ranks, but it hadn't made them go away. When the intercom buzzed, he walked back to his desk and picked up the receiver.

"Mr. Halstrom to see you, sir," announced the receptionist.

"Tell him to come right in," he ordered, and waited for the door to open.

"Any breakthroughs?" Demarist asked without turning around to look at his plant manager.

"Bogged down is more like it," said Phil Halstrom.

"Why the hell won't they listen to reason? The union knows the position we're in. The company can't afford the extra benefits they're asking for. I pay them enough, don't I?"

"Pay isn't the issue, Quince. We settled that two weeks ago. But they know that the business forecasts are good, so they're asking for a larger slice of the profit pie."

"What should I tell our negotiators, then?"

"Tell them to walk out and get back to their desks. They have enough other work to keep them busy for a couple of weeks yet." Looking back through the blinds, Demarist added, "Maybe a few more days out there will soften them up a bit."

❄ ❄ ❄

"Anything new at the plant, Quince?" asked Valerie as her husband entered the house.

"Don't ask," he said, dropping himself into the closest chair.

Valerie walked up behind him and massaged the back of his neck. "I can always tell when you're tense. The strain shows on your face."

"That feels good," he said, closing his eyes and relaxing. "You always know what to do. I wish I did."

"No progress, right?" she guessed.

"For the first time in twenty years we have a chance to make some larger profits. We could expand or diversify. Buy up some smaller companies in other market sectors. Then we wouldn't be so dependent on our own business. But the union's demands would really put the squelch on that."

"You're getting tense again, I can feel it," she admonished. "At least tonight you can forget about it."

"What's tonight?"

"Jennifer's Penance preparation meeting."

"I thought it was next week."

"Next week there's one too."

"Why all these meetings? We didn't have to go through all this when Justin and Alex made their first confessions."

"That was over ten years ago," she said.

"Who would have thought we'd have another one so much later," Quincy smiled. He reached up and put his hand on Valerie's. "She's kept me young, a real bright spot, being a daddy again."

"She's kept us both young...and involved with the parish. I think they've got more going for kids than they do for adults."

"Just as well. I wouldn't have the time, anyway," said Quincy.

"Time for what, Daddy?" asked Jennifer, peeking around the doorjamb.

"Hi, there, Funch!" said her father, turning around while Valerie went to check the oven. "Funch" was the nickname he and Valerie had used for Jennifer since her birth. The name came from Funchal in the Madeira Islands where Quincy and Valerie had been vacationing when Jennifer was most likely conceived.

"Daddy, stop calling me that. It sounds like 'lunch,' " said Jennifer. The name had started to embarrass her. She was getting too old for it.

"Time for a kiss," said Quincy as he reached out to hug his little girl. "And then," he added, "time for our meeting tonight."

❄ ❄ ❄

"Thank you all for coming to the meeting tonight," Mrs. Lucas began in the cafeteria at St. Joseph's. Parents and children filled the room. "Every year we consider moving our first confession program to a warmer month, but in the Church's liturgical year it seems to fit best in Advent. This way we can end our program with the Advent reconciliation service."

Quincy leaned toward his wife and whispered, "What's a reconciliation service?"

"Shh. You'll see. I went last year," Valerie reminded him.

"One purpose of all the sacrament preparation programs here at St. Joseph's is to provide some theological updating for parents. You're all busy people, I know, and our parish has not been so successful in offering adult education programs for their own sake. Many of you are professional people, though, and you know you have to keep up with the latest trends if you want to do well in your work. Success in parenting is also important, and we all want to do well in our daily lives. So in these programs we try to offer ideas not just for your children but for yourselves — ideas that will keep you abreast of developments in the Church, and that will be helpful in your own life."

"Who does she think she is, a priest?" mumbled Quincy.

"She's the parish religious education director," answered his wife. "Now be quiet."

Mrs. Lucas continued, "I'll be with you this week to give you some contemporary insights into the meaning of repentance and conversion. Then you'll have a chance to share with one another what you've learned. By the way, for those of you who don't know me well, I do have a master's degree in theology. I tell you that to reassure you that what I'm saying here this evening is accurate Church theology. Next week Father Boyd will be our speaker, and he'll touch more on the liturgical aspects of Reconciliation."

"At least she's leaving the priesting up to the priest," Quincy commented.

"And at least we sat in the back where she can't hear you," Valerie whispered.

"Many of us grow up with the idea," Mrs. Lucas continued, "that sin is simply committing a bad action. We hear a lot of talk about 'committing sins,' and there's some truth to that. In the religious education classes that your children are attending, we've spent quite a bit of time with that this year, haven't we, kids?"

Small heads nodded in assent.

"We read about Adam and Eve and the sin that they committed, and how they alienated themselves from God and one another as a result. Kids can really relate to that, since they often get punished for doing things they shouldn't. How many of you can tell me what the sin was that they committed?"

Hands shot up.

"Carl?"

"Eating an apple."

"People often picture it as an apple, but the Bible story just says it was a fruit. But eating a fruit isn't bad in itself. Why was this a sin? Cecilia?"

"Because God told them not to do it."

"In other words, the real sin was one of disobedience. The sin of disobedience can be a real problem for you guys, can't it?" said Mrs. Lucas to the children, "especially since so often it can be hard to see *why* something is wrong."

A chorus of yeses came back from the children. Quincy found himself thinking about the strikers down at the plant and how they were disobeying management's orders.

"You just know *that* it's wrong, and if you do wrong you will probably get punished." She addressed the parents again. "From that reward and punishment outlook we then take the children into the world of the Ten Commandments, which at first glance seems to be more of the same. God seems to be saying, 'Do this and don't do that or else you're going to be punished.' How many of you kids think you can remember all ten of the commandments?"

A few hands shot into the air as if to say, "Please pick me, Mrs. Lucas, *please*." A few other hands crept up cautiously.

"Good!" she said. "That's fine. We don't need to go over them here, because I'm sure your parents remember them all."

The grown-ups in the room got caught a little off guard, but before they could say yes or no, the teacher continued speaking to the children.

"Why did God give the Jewish people these laws? Was it just to give them more rules, so if they broke them they would be punished? Who remembers what you learned in class? Jamie?"

"So that they would be happier."

"Right. And why would they be happier? Jennifer?"

"Because they would be nicer to one another. If they obeyed the commandments God gave them, they could stay friends."

Quincy felt his grumpiness turn to pride over his daughter's correct answer.

"Very good," said Mrs. Lucas. "If we lie, cheat, and steal from one another, we can't stay friends for very long. And if we respect our parents and give honor to God, we have a good relationship with them." She turned her attention to the parents again. "What we've learned in religion class, then, and what I've just been reviewing with you is that much of the morality in the Old Testament is really about relationships, even though at first glance it looks like it's about laws and rules.

"That insight is one of the key contributions of recent scholarship to the nature of biblical morality. Sin was not so much a breaking of a rule as much as it was a breakdown in a relationship — between God and people or between people and one another. One scriptural word for that relationship is *covenant*. We read in the Bible about how God made a covenant with Noah and another one with Abraham and another one with Moses and the Israelites. With each covenant, God drew people into a closer relationship with him and made them promise to live in better relationships with one another.

"But what happens when the covenant gets broken? What happens when somebody does something that breaks down the relationship? First, someone has to notice that the relationship is not what it's supposed to be. Second, somebody has to change, has to turn around, has to do something to mend the relationship.

"Kids, who did we learn were the people in the Old Testament who told the Israelites when they had done something to break the covenant? Francine?"

"The prophets."

"Yes, the prophets have been called 'the conscience of Israel.' They were people with a keen moral sense of right and wrong. When they saw the Israelites doing something wrong — like worshiping false gods made of gold and silver — they told them to do something. Who remembers what it was? Carl, you have your hand up again."

"Repent!" Carl hollered.

The parents laughed. "Hey, he's pretty good!" one father said.

"I just knew Carl would get that one," said Mrs. Lucas. "I think he's practicing to be a prophet when he grows up. He warns his classmates to 'Repent!' when they're doing something bad. He even caught me one day after school as I was scolding my daughter. Thank you, Carl, I needed that.

"And we all need that. We all need reminders from time to time of how we might be hurting relationships in our lives. We need them from our parents as we're growing up and from friends who care enough about us to tell us if we're messing things up as we get older. If we marry, a spouse can be a gentle prophet to us, telling us when we need to change and what we need to do to set things right. We all need prophetic voices in our lives if our relationships with others are to grow and stay healthy.

"When the biblical prophets said 'Repent!' they were telling people to change their minds and change their hearts. They had broken the covenant; they had done something to spoil their relationship with God or with someone else in their society. So the prophets told them that they had to turn around and mend the relationship. In other words, seek reconciliation.

"Reconciliation is thus a better word to use than 'confession' if we want to express what this sacrament is all about, which is why the name was changed when the Church revised its rituals in the 1970s. Like the prophets in Israel, the Church has always recognized that people need to turn away from whatever might be hurting their relationships with God and others. During the first centuries of Christianity, there was a ritual of public repentance for those who committed serious crimes. In the Middle Ages, private confession became the principal sacrament of repentance in the Church, and it's been that way ever since.

"But whether repentance is done in public or private, the purpose of the Church's sacrament is the same. It's to give people an opportunity to look at their lives and see what might be going wrong in their relationships. Sometimes the Church has sounded legalistic about this. That's because in the past most people thought of morality in terms of laws you shouldn't break and commandments you shouldn't disobey. Today, however, with the help of biblical scholarship and from psychology and sociology, we have more insight into the nature of morality as relationship.

"If this sounds abstract, it's because it is! I've been trying to condense into just a few minutes the past few weeks of religious instruction that your children have been receiving.

"That's not the way we teach in the classes, though. And it's not the way that Jesus taught. Jesus taught much of what he had to tell us in parables or stories. One of the best-known and loved parables that Jesus told is the parable of the Prodigal Son. Which of you boys and girls can tell us the story? Emily?"

"A boy asks his father for some money that he's going to inherit anyway. The father gives it to him, and the boy…I guess he really must be a little older than that…well, anyway, the son goes away and spends all the money and doesn't have any left. He tries to make it on his own, but all he can get are rotten jobs. Finally he decides to go back home and see if he can work for his father instead. But his father doesn't hire him. Instead he throws a big party and welcomes him back to the family as a son."

"And…what happens next?" the teacher asked.

"Oh, yes. Then the boy's older brother gets jealous. He's mad because he's been a good son all his life and his father never threw such a big party for him. But the father tells him not to be jealous because he loves them both so much."

"A very good summary. Thanks, Emily. Earlier this evening I said you'd all have a chance to discuss this a bit with one another, but before we do that I'd like to do something to make the story more vivid in our minds. It's a Teleketics film called *The Way Home,* and it's sort of an updated version of that parable. If we might have the lights out."

As parents and children shifted in their seats, Quincy caught sight of a familiar face. "My God, do you see who's here?" he said to his wife.

"Who?" she asked.

"It's Dave Santucci, the union shop steward," he said, trying to hide behind the woman sitting in front of him.

"I know Mr. Santucci," said Jennifer. "He's a nice man. Why don't you want him to see you?"

"Shh," said Valerie to her daughter. "Your father and he are not on the best of terms right now. Mr. Santucci is leading the strike at the factory. He's asking for things that would cost us more money."

"But we have lots of money, don't we, Daddy?" Jennifer asked innocently.

"I think the movie's starting," said Quincy, avoiding the question.

Music poured out of the speaker, drowning out any more possible questions from Jennifer, much to Quincy's relief.

When the movie ended, Mrs. Lucas began speaking again. "The facts of the story are fairly simple, and the comparisons with the Scripture parable are pretty obvious so we need not discuss them. I do think it would be good, though, to focus on the feelings of the three main characters, and the feelings they arouse in us. If sin and repentance are not just facts but matters of relationship, we can get a better sense of how relationships are broken and mended by getting in touch with the feelings that come with them.

"I would like you now to get in groups of about six people, which tonight would mean two or three children with the parent or parents who brought them. Many times families don't take the time to discuss feelings because we're so busy talking about other things. Usually we don't get many chances to learn from other families because we're so caught up in our own. Tonight, then, I'd like to create the opportunity for you to do something different and to learn at a deeper level than just the intellectual one.

"Children, you needn't feel outclassed by your parents; very often grown-ups have as hard a time with this as you do. And parents, you needn't feel shy about doing this; I chose this learning experience so that you and your children could enter into it on the same level. We're all in this together."

As the children and their parents arranged their chairs in circles, Quincy breathed a sigh of relief when he saw that Santucci was in a different discussion group on the other side of the room.

When everyone settled down, Mrs. Lucas continued. "Your task as a group will be to share your answers to these two questions: First, how do you think each of the characters felt at different points in the story? Second, what was one time in your life when you yourself felt that way? If you do that three times, once for the younger son, once for the older son, and once for the father in the story, it should take us pretty close to the end of our time together."

When the groups had finished, they turned their chairs around again to listen to Mrs. Lucas. "Sometimes when I use that film in religious education, I ask people which of the three characters they identify with. Most people identify with the older son. Ask yourselves this on your way home tonight: Which of the characters do you most often feel like, and why? Actually, Jesus told that story so his listeners could learn to identify more with the younger son, the one who sees he has done something to hurt his father and then returns to ask forgiveness. This is why it is a story of repentance and reconciliation. All too often we either don't see the bad situation our selfishness has caused or, if we do, we're too stubborn to turn around and try to make things better.

"Also, most of us see the father in the story as a God figure, since we know that God cares for us and forgives us. But we forget that Jesus asked his followers to be like God in this respect, that is, to care about others and seek reconciliation wherever it is needed. That's what Jesus meant by overcoming the sin of the world. He wanted us to overcome our separation from others and get back into good, healthy, and caring relationships with them.

"The sacrament of Reconciliation is one of the opportunities the Church provides for us to become more like the repentant son or the forgiving father. Next week Father Boyd will describe for us the various ways this can happen."

❋   ❋   ❋

During the drive home, Jennifer broke the silence by saying, "I don't care what Mrs. Lucas says. Most times I feel like the *younger* son. When I do something wrong, *I'm* the one who has to say I'm sorry. What about you, Mom and Dad? Which one do *you* most often feel like?"

After a moment's thought, Valerie said, "I suppose that's one of the advantages of being a youngster — as you get older it sometimes gets harder to turn around and admit you're wrong."

Quincy said nothing and just kept driving through the snow.

❋   ❋   ❋

Two days later a warm front moved in. The snow turned to slush, and the number of strikers outside the plant doubled. Quincy looked up from his desk and let his gaze drift out the office window. It was hard to concentrate on the few papers he had to work on. Nothing much to do these days except watch back orders pile up. Quincy had outsmarted the strikers by working overtime to build up his inventory for the Christmas rush. His fourth quarter earnings would not be that far off from last year's.

The intercom buzzed; this time it was Halstrom, coming in to give his midafternoon report.

"Well, how'd it go today?" he asked, pretending to be busy with the file on his desk.

"The plant's fine. Floors are swept. Security just double-checked the alarm system — something they've been meaning to do for months. It's amazing what you can do when you have the time," said the plant manager, trying to be upbeat.

"I meant with the negotiations," scowled his boss.

"Quince, you know there aren't any negotiations. Just some guys looking across a table at one another for a couple of hours every day. What a way to earn a paycheck."

"I'm only paying half of them," corrected the president. "The ones on our side of the table."

"Even so, there's not much they can do unless we give them some bargaining chips," he suggested.

"What do you want me to do, give the business away? I built this business up from when we started in a garage, buying up wire overstock and figuring out what we could make out of it. Ran every machine by hand, not semiautomated the way we have it now."

"I know. I've seen you build up this business from scratch. I'm the only plant manager this company's ever had, after you. I just hate seeing you losing it."

"Losing it? We've got plenty of cash reserves, Phil. I'm not about to lose this plant."

"I don't mean the building, I mean the company. The company's not just the factory. It's the people who work here too. It's not like the old days. You're losing them."

"Meaning…?"

"Meaning in the beginning everybody pulled together to get the business off the ground. I stayed after hours filling orders. Line workers put in overtime without getting paid time and a half."

"That was before the union came in and took over," Quincy reminded him.

"Just before the first strike too," Phil added.

"But we beat 'em every time," Demarist reflected. "Every time they got less than half of what they asked for."

"That's not the way I look at it. Sure, our output has gone up almost every year. But after every strike, our productivity per hour has gone down. People don't feel like working as hard after they've been beaten. Every time we 'win,' we lose. We lose in productivity, we lose in company loyalty…."

"Whose side are you on anyway, Halstrom?"

"I'm on your side, Quince. Without you, I wouldn't be where I am today. You and the company have really helped me out, what with helping me earn my bachelor's degree and M.B.A. But I've also worked with the folks downstairs for almost twenty years. I know what they're feeling. This time you're losing them again, possibly for the last time."

"I can fire the whole damn lot of them and start from scratch again!" Demarist insisted.

"And then what becomes of your dream of expansion and diversification?" Phil knew he had struck a nerve.

"Are you telling me how to run this business?" Quincy preferred offensive to defensive strategies.

"I'm just trying to speak to you as a friend."

"Some friend you're turning out to be!"

"Look, Quince, it's almost Christmas. The union thought this would all be over by now. They've got their strike fund, but it doesn't give them full pay. Even the office staff is down over the announcement that Christmas bonuses will be canceled if the strike isn't over soon. I hear people talking about looking for jobs elsewhere. You're losing them."

"So what am I supposed to do? Give in?"

"Just give me something I can negotiate with. Stop taking such a hard line on the benefits issue. Say at least you're willing to listen. What good does it do you if we win this fight but lose the heart and soul of your company?"

"Who do you think you are, a prophet?" Demarist barked.

Phil Halstrom's face scrunched up in puzzlement. "What's *that* supposed to mean?"

"Nothing. Forget it."

❆   ❆   ❆

"Jennifer, eat your broccoli," Valerie Demarist said as she picked at her own food.

"I'm not hungry, Mom."

"Do as your mother says, Funch," Quincy added.

"I'm *not* 'Funch'! How many times do I have to tell you that!" Embarrassed and angry, the girl pushed herself away from the table and ran up to her room.

"What's got into her?" asked Quincy.

"She's upset because Becky Carroll's moving away," Valerie informed him.

"I know they've been friends for years, but…"

Valerie interrupted him. "They started school together. She was Jennifer's first friend in school," his wife tried to explain.

"Jennifer's got other friends. She makes friends easily," Quincy said, lightly dismissing the issue.

Valerie waited awhile, not looking up from her plate. "That's not all of it," she said at last. "Becky told her that her father decided to look for a new job as soon as the negotiations broke down." Looking up, she added, "Tim Carroll works for you. At least he used to."

"This damn small town!" hollered Quincy. He slammed his fork down on the table. "I should have moved the company to Detroit when I had the chance last year. Then everybody and their brother wouldn't know us and we wouldn't know them….I suppose Jennifer's blaming me for losing her friend?"

"That's the way it looks to her, I guess."

"Jeez," he said. "Why does she have to take it so *personally?*"

❄   ❄   ❄

The Demarists sat near the rear of the cafeteria again at the next meeting. This time Valerie sat between her husband and daughter, acting as a demilitarized zone between the two.

Father Toby Boyd had only been at St. Joseph's a couple of months, and it was only his second assignment after ordination. His first had been in Grand Rapids, but when the pastor suffered a mild stroke, Father Boyd came in to help run the small parish. He hadn't completely adjusted to his new setting yet.

"I apologize for not knowing many of you," the young priest began, "but filling in for Monsignor Kendall has taken a good deal of my time. He and Mrs. Lucas have worked closely in developing the sacrament preparation programs here at St. Joseph's, and normally he would have been giving you this talk instead of me. He's had a lot more experience in hearing confessions than I have. Mrs. Lucas has filled me in on what you did last week at the meeting, and I hope that what I share with you tonight will be helpful not only for the young people here but for everyone.

"I say that quite aware that it's not just children who need to become acquainted with the sacrament of Reconciliation. Don't get me wrong — I'm not going to try and drive any of you back to frequent confession. In the past ten or twenty years, at least in the United States, the Church's whole approach to the sacrament has changed. And when I speak of the Church, I don't mean the hierarchy. This change has come from the bottom up, from the people who *are* the Church. Change of this sort is really nothing new in the Church. Mrs. Lucas told me that last week she mentioned the practice of public repentance in the early centuries of Christianity. The practice of confessing sins declined not because the bishops ordered it but because *people* didn't like the humiliation that often accompanied it. Private confession developed in the Middle Ages, not because the bishops ordered it but because the *people* in the Church felt a need for forgiveness by God, and in their eyes the priest stood for God. Eventually, what the Church was doing was approved by the bishops.

"In our own century, we're witnessing the same sort of change. People in the Church have taken what used to be a weekly or monthly practice and made it a much more infrequent practice. What used to be just a recitation of a list of sins has now become an examination of sinfulness. People have taken what used to be fairly ordinary and made it into something very special. At least, that's the way I look at it. Maybe I look at it that way because I've been a layman in the Church much longer than I've had a chance to be a priest yet!

"To be fair to the Church's leaders, though, you have to admit that the changes in this sacrament have not all come from the bottom up. One of the big changes came from the scholars and theologians in the Church who helped us see that sin is more than just breaking the commandments. As Mrs. Lucas pointed out last week, the tragedy of sin is the breakdown of relationships that it causes. It alienates people from God and from one another. When people no longer listen to God, they get out of touch with the goodness and the beauty of life because God is the source of everything that makes us really happy. The same thing happens when people no longer reach out to one another. They become isolated and alone…in need of reconciliation."

Valerie glanced at Quincy as he rubbed the back of his neck.

"In recent years," Father Boyd continued, "scholars and theologians have helped us see that there are more dimensions to sin than we used to think. We've always known about personal sins like doing things that hurt others, ourselves, or our relationship with God. But we never used to think much about the social dimension of sin — the ripple effect our selfish acts can have on other people, even on people we don't even know. Many times when we commit social sins we don't even know that we're committing them.

"One reason that we often don't see the sinfulness of social sin is that everybody does it, and so it seems normal, not sinful. They say that even the Mafia has a code of honor, but what the gangsters in the Mob don't see is that their whole code is rife with sin. Sometimes we Americans don't see that the way we treat other countries is hurting them while it is benefiting us. Or sometimes we do business in a way that is unfair, unjust, mean, or careless — all in the name of making a buck. We then justify it by saying that 'everybody does it.'

"But sometimes social sin, like personal sin, is not something that we do but something that we *don't* do. On the personal level, it can be not spending time with your children, not being attentive to your spouse, not listening to your parents. All of those failings hurt the relationships people have with others. On the social level, it can be not caring about the needs of others or not doing anything to change a situation in which people are hurting. We can easily see this in the way that citizens of Nazi Germany did nothing to prevent the extermination of Jews, but we usually don't see it in the Americans who did nothing about the extermination of native American Indians. Invisible sin is far more widespread than we used to realize.

"By giving us deeper, and sometimes more painful, insights into our own sinfulness, scholars and theologians have encouraged us to take the meaning of Reconciliation much more seriously than we used to. We used to think that it was enough to tell our sins to a priest and be forgiven by God. Now we often realize that we should not go to confession unless we are ready to experience conversion and seek reconciliation with others as well as with God.

"The bishops in the Church have also contributed greatly to recent changes in the practice of confession. I suppose that's one reason why I see these changes as the work of the Holy Spirit inspiring the whole Church from bottom to top in the renewal of this sacrament. At the Second Vatican Council, the bishops approved changes in the form of the sacrament just before most people realized that the old form needed to be changed.

"Actually, there are now three forms of the sacrament of Reconciliation. Let me take the third one first, since that one is probably the least familiar to you.

"Let's suppose you are a priest leading a group of Catholic pilgrims on a tour of the Holy Land, and suddenly your bus is ambushed by terrorists. The tires have been shot out, and you're not sure what's going to happen next. People are wondering if they are going to die. While you're stuck there in the uncertain silence, you ask if anyone wants to go to confession and half the hands in the bus go up. There's no privacy to hear individual confessions and maybe no time for that. What do you do?

"Or let's suppose you are the bishop of a mission territory, and you don't have many priests. There are thousands of Catholics in thousands of square miles but only a handful of priests, and each one has to travel by Jeep to four missions every weekend to say Mass. There's no time to listen to confessions every weekend. What do you do?

"In this second case, the bishop could make a pastoral decision that each priest should stay over in the last mission he visits every week, and by rotating where he stays he could hear confessions in each place once every four weeks. On the other three weekends, he would celebrate what is called the Rite of Reconciliation With General Confession and Absolution. It is a liturgical service in which the priest reads from the Scriptures and gives a brief talk. Then he invites people to confess their sins to God in their hearts, and assures them they have God's love and forgiveness for their sins.

"In the first case, the priest could make an emergency decision to do something like this on his own, even without a bishop's permission. Even if he didn't have time for a Scripture reading and homily, he could ask all those who wished to be absolved from their sins to seek the Lord's forgiveness in the silence of their hearts, and then he would bless them and assure them that their sins are forgiven.

"In both cases, however, the priest would make it clear to the people that if any sin they confessed in silence was very serious, they ought to see a priest when they get a chance. He encourages this not because they need to have their sins forgiven again but to continue the process of reconciliation.

"By very serious sins I mean what used to be called 'mortal sins,' or things we decide to do that prevent us from having any kind of relationship with God. Decisions like that put a wall of separation between us and God and literally kill the life of the Spirit in our hearts. As you might gather, most people do not commit too many mortal sins in their lives, and if they do they usually turn back to God. But all of us are sinners and in need of reconciliation to some extent. That's why we should still take advantage of the sacrament of Reconciliation when it is available.

"The second form of the sacrament of Reconciliation is one which seems to have become standard practice in the Church today. It is a liturgical service that combines the features of the general form with the opportunity for people to confess individually. Many parishes now have these penitential services during Lent and Advent and a few other times during the year, as may be needed.

"A reconciliation service begins with Scripture readings and a homily or instruction by the priest. In this talk he usually tries to help the people examine their relationship with God and the other people in their lives. After that, those who want to seek Reconciliation through the priest can usually choose to go to one of several who are available.

"Sometimes people may choose to use the traditional confession booth because they are familiar with it and because it contains a screen that helps them remain anonymous. Sometimes, however, people may choose to use the reconciliation room, which is more like a little office in which the person and the priest can sit and talk things over face-to-face. More and more people these days prefer the room to the confessional. When the religion teachers took the children to look at both of them in the church a few weeks ago, I needn't tell you which one the kids preferred!

"Years ago there used to be a set formula for beginning your confession to the priest, which began, 'Bless me, Father, for I have sinned,' but that is not required today. Now you can just talk to the priest as you would to any other person, telling him what is weighing on your soul. Then he'll talk to you a bit, reminding you of God's love and mercy, and perhaps offering some counseling or other advice.

He will also ask you to do something to show your change of heart and your renewed commitment to living the way Christ wants us to. This may take the form of praying or meditating on a passage from the Scriptures in order to come closer to the Lord. Or it may take the form of doing something to overcome a problem in your life or to help you become reconciled with others. Before you leave, he will give you his blessing and assure you of God's forgiveness in absolving your sins.

"Finally, after everyone has had a chance to go to confession, the penance service ends with a prayer of thanks and a blessing over all the people. Sometimes, however, if the number of people going to confession is so large that it will obviously be a long time before everyone is finished, this final ceremony is omitted.

"That leaves just one more form of the sacrament, which is the Rite of Reconciliation for Individual Penitents. If you go to confession on your own, and there is no special service for the people, this is the form that's used. People used to go to confession regularly on Saturdays, but now more often they'll go when they are on a retreat, or when they go to a priest to discuss specific problems they might also ask him to hear their confessions.

"This rite is very much like the penance service, except that it is quite individualized. After greeting the person, the priest might say a prayer or read a passage from the Bible. After hearing the person's confession and offering the same kind of advice and counseling as I mentioned before, the priest might pray individually with the person before saying the words of absolution and giving his blessing. This form of the sacrament is very adaptable to the circumstances in which it is used.

"As you can see, then, the changes in the liturgical form of the sacrament and options among the different rites are very compatible with the changes in our growing understanding of sin, repentance, and reconciliation. Many people now say that although they go to confession less frequently than they used to, when they celebrate the sacrament it has more meaning than it used to the old way. And I have also heard older priests say that it is personally more rewarding and spiritually more enriching for them to hear confessions now than it used to be.

"Well, that's the end of my prepared remarks. Are there any

questions? I apologize that I won't be able to recognize you by name. Yes — in the middle, the gentleman with his hand up."

"You said that people don't go to confession as often as they used to. Isn't there a Church law that says you have to go to confession at least once a year?"

"Actually, the rule is that if you commit a very serious mortal sin you should not let a year go by without going to confession. But if you have never seriously broken your relationship with God or the Church, there is no strict obligation for you to go to confession as long as you are in the 'state of grace,' as we say. Even though you may not need the sacrament to return to spiritual life, however, it is always helpful for spiritual growth.

"Next? Yes, the lady here in front."

"What about the seal of confession? That's still in effect, isn't it, even with all these changes?"

"Oh, definitely. The seal of confession is the priest's strict obligation never to reveal anything he has heard in confession. The priest is sworn to absolute secrecy, and no one can make him talk about what a person has told him in strictest confidence — not the police, not the courts, not even the pope!"

Quincy found the last point reassuring. He did not think very much about it, though. Other things occupied his mind. Besides the strike, now his daughter had turned icy on him. She had always been cute little Funch. What was wrong with her?

❉   ❉   ❉

Quincy mumbled to himself. "There's nothing I can do to change the situation. Tim Carroll and his family will move regardless of what happens at the factory now. Why can't Jennifer listen to reason? Even that new priest with all his fancy talk about reconciliation couldn't do anything. I've tried to say I'm sorry, but she just doesn't hear me."

Lately, the only person who'd smiled at him was his receptionist, but she was paid to do that. Even the daily meetings with Halstrom had been cut out, to save the strain on both of them. The closer it got to Christmas, the less he wanted to have anything to do with the factory.

"A penny for your thoughts," Valerie said, trying to be nice, as she entered the bedroom. Her voice startled him.

"I was just thinking about Christmas — about Jennifer and Christmas. If she doesn't come around, I'm not going to enjoy it one bit. You and she are all I have now."

"You have your health. You have your sons and your grandchildren," she said, trying to be positive. "You have your business...."

"Phil was right. I don't have the business anymore. I might have an ulcer, though."

"Don't say that!" she reprimanded. "Why do you say that?"

"Sorry. I didn't mean to scare you. My stomach's been upset the past few days. I guess I was just wondering out loud."

"Is it worth an ulcer?" she asked.

"What's worth an ulcer?" he parried.

"This matter of the strike. What would it cost you if you gave in?" Her question was genuinely curious. Quincy never discussed matters of business with her, at least not in detail.

"If the union got half of what it's asking for, it would cut our anticipated profits by a third. That would mean five more years before we could really expand or diversify. I'm not willing to wait that long."

"I thought you once said something about the pay raises already being settled," she went on, exploring.

"Well, if you want the whole damned laundry list," he began with new energy in his voice, "I'll give it to you. There isn't much else to talk about these days, anyway."

Quincy immediately felt guilty about hollering at his wife. She was the only person who had never spoken harshly to him. At the same time he felt oddly happy — as though he were about to break through some kind of invisible barrier. Valerie just listened.

"It's a list of fringe benefits. The union's mounted a two-pronged attack. On the one hand they want more days off with pay, including more sick leave and even time off when their wives have babies! The women *already* get maternity leave. I don't see why men should need it. Then they want increased medical coverage, including full outpatient and dental care for their families. They're already covered with hospitalization for themselves. Plus there's workmen's comp and unemployment insurance I have to pay. Why can't they be satisfied with what they've got? I've been a good employer all these years. I obey all the minimum government regulations."

"Is that it?" she asked, surprised that the list seemed so short.

"That's the quickie version of it. If you want all the details, you have to consult a lawyer, the way I do. But the bottom line is still the same."

"I don't know how to say this to you, Quince. I'm not a lawyer. I'm not even a businesswoman. But I don't hear them asking for anything we don't have. I mean ourselves — our family."

"That's just the point. I've worked hard for twenty years to get us where we are. Some of these jerks have never put in more than an eight-hour day. Some of them are kids fresh out of high school. They haven't even worked a full year yet. Why should they have what I've worked day and night for for twenty years?" Quincy had rehearsed those arguments in his head many times. Now they were out in the open for the first time.

"I appreciate all you've done for us, dear," Valerie said, trying to find some way around the impasse. "But would they have to get it all at once?" she tried. "Couldn't they get a little at a time, the longer they worked for the company or something?"

"The union wouldn't go for that," Quincy dismissed the idea.

"Have you asked them?"

"I know what they would say."

"Why don't you ask them?"

Quincy said nothing for a moment. He wanted to be honest with the woman who loved him. "I don't know, Val. I just don't know."

❄   ❄   ❄

In the still night clusters of snowflakes floated down into the light cast by the street lamps. Outside St. Joseph's Church the earth slept, silent under the blanket of new snow that made the dirtiest of streets appear to be immaculate.

Inside, Mrs. Lucas lit three candles in the Advent wreath.

The Demarists seated themselves in a middle pew. Perhaps it was because Quincy had led them halfway down the aisle before realizing where he was. Perhaps it was because Valerie had noticed the Santucci family sitting in the back.

The Reconciliation service began with Father Boyd reading from the Gospel according to John 14:23-27:

Jesus answered and said to him, "Whoever loves me will keep my word, and my Father will love him, and we will come to him and make our dwelling with him. Whoever does not love me does not keep my words; yet the word you hear is not mine but that of the Father who sent me.

I have told you this while I am with you. The Advocate, the holy Spirit that the Father will send in my name — he will teach you everything and remind you of all that [I] told you. Peace I leave with you; my peace I give to you. Not as the world gives do I give it to you. Do not let your hearts be troubled or afraid.

Monsignor Kendall rose from his seat to speak from the pulpit. "These words of our Lord, spoken shortly before his death, are quite appropriate for this Advent season in which we prepare for the celebration of his birth. His birth brought mankind the promise of new life, and his death enabled that promise to come true.

"Our theme this evening is 'The Advent of New Life.' That new life is life lived in his Spirit. It is the Spirit of love — a love of caring and consideration for others. It is the Spirit of peace, both peace within our own hearts and peace with our neighbors. It is, you could even say, the Spirit of Christmas.

"But the Holy Spirit is also the Spirit of truth. If we listen to the Spirit speaking in our own conscience, God teaches us right from wrong. The right way to God's life is a way of loving, caring, and giving. It leads to peace. The wrong way leads to war — war within ourselves, war with others, war with God. Sometimes it is a hot war, sometimes a cold war. But it is not peace.

"Sometimes, strange as it seems, we prefer war to peace. We prefer the way things are, the way *we* are. The conversion that would open up the road to peace for us seems threatening. We do not want to change. We are afraid to change. Yet Jesus tells us, 'Do not let your hearts be troubled or afraid.'

"We find God's words of life in many places in the Scriptures. But two in particular are most appropriate as we examine our conscience in preparation for the sacrament of Reconciliation: the Ten Commandments and the Beatitudes.

"The commandments are God's words spoken to the Israelites; the Beatitudes are Christ's words spoken to his disciples. The commandments tell us what we should *not* do; the Beatitudes tell us what we *should* do. The commandments give us the minimum requirements for living God's life; the Beatitudes show us the ideals we ought to aim toward for living fully in the Spirit.

"To prepare for the worthy celebration of the sacrament, therefore, let us briefly review these guides to help us live a loving, holy life. And as we listen, let us ask: Have we chosen the path to peace? And if not, will we open the door to reconciliation?

"First, the commandments.

"Have I given God the honor which is due to him? Have I worshiped other gods of gold and silver, power and ambition, fame and success? Have I kept holy the day which he has set aside as a day of rest? Have I worshiped him as I ought to?

"Have I honored my parents? Have I shown respect to all those who deserve my respect? Have I treated my brothers and my sisters the way Jesus wants me to?

"Have I killed anyone — with my tongue, if not with my hands? Have I killed their love for me or crushed their hopes or destroyed their self-respect? Have I hit anyone in anger? Have I caused anyone harm in any way? Have I fully respected human life, even the life of an unborn child?

"Have I physically taken anything that was not mine? Have I taken credit for something I did not do, robbing someone else of the praise that they deserved? Have I been fair to people, not taking more than what they owed me and giving them all that they deserved? Have I been envious or greedy or selfish? Have I used more than I need while others do not have the bare necessities?

"Have I lied or said anything untrue so that it would be to my advantage? Have I hurt someone else's reputation or tarnished their good name? Have I gossiped or passed on rumors without checking the facts or source? Have I believed or approved of slanderous talk about others without regard for the truth?

"Have I been faithful to my husband or wife? Have I loved my spouse the way that he or she deserves and needs to be loved? Have I respected my own body and the bodies of others the way that God wants me to? Have I persuaded someone into being unfaithful to their spouse or to their own integrity?

"As I said earlier, those are the minimums. To live God's life to the fullest, we must also listen to the Beatitudes.

"Am I poor in spirit, if not in wealth? Do I share what I have with those who have less?

"Am I gentle with others and with myself? Am I kind, considerate, and caring, not just sometimes but as a way of life?

"Do I mourn with others, share their grief, suffer their pain? Do I listen to them when they need to speak? Do I stand by them in their hour of darkness and give them hope?

"Do I hunger for what is right? Do I thirst for justice? Do I work to right the wrongs in society? Do I strive to give everyone an equal opportunity in life?

"Am I merciful? Do I forgive others for what they have done? Do I forgive them not once but over and over again? Do I forgive not only those who like me but also my enemies?

"Am I pure in heart? Or are my motives mixed? Do I wish only the best for others? Do I see God in them?

"Am I a peacemaker? Do I do what is needed to bring about good relationships between the people I live with, the children I go to school with, the people I work with? Do I contribute to the effort to bring an end to the arms race?

"Do I work so hard for justice and peace that I am persecuted, mocked, called an idealist, a traitor, a coward, or a liberal? Am I willing to risk all that I have, the way Jesus did, for peace on earth?

"There you have them — the Ten Commandments and the Beatitudes, the minimums and the maximums, the basic requirements and the ideal goals for living in the Spirit. We all fall short of the ideal, but Jesus calls us to it. We sometimes miss even the basics, but help is always available if we will only turn to God and ask for it.

"Let us pray...." Monsignor Kendall led the congregation in asking God for enlightenment and discernment in the examination of conscience and for forgiveness of sins both remembered and forgotten. After leading the Lord's Prayer, he concluded with the words: "God, our source of life, you know our weakness. May we reach out with joy to grasp your hand and walk more readily in your ways. We ask this through Christ our Lord. Amen."

After inviting everyone to take advantage of the sacrament, the pastor pointed out the places where the priests would be available for confession. One by one, children, parents, and other parishioners began to rise and move in the four directions. Others waited, preferring to sit or kneel in the pews before going to confession or preferring just to pray before leaving.

Jennifer left the Demarist family first. A short while later, Valerie rose from her husband's side. After looking around, she chose the traditional confessional. J. Quincy Demarist sat by himself and watched the people of all shapes and sizes coming and going. One of the guitarists plucked a soft tune and hummed. The air smelled of burning candles and various ladies' perfumes mingling with one another. Quincy put his hand on the edge of the old oak pew in front of him. The pews had been there since the church was built around the turn of the century. As he felt the smooth rubbed wood he wondered how many other men had felt the same wood, knelt on the same kneeler, prayed to the same God for an answer, help, and forgiveness when it seemed there was none to be found.

Jennifer returned to the pew. She kissed Quincy on the cheek and said softly, "I love you, Daddy."

Taken aback, Quincy turned to her and whispered, "What's that all about?"

His daughter sat down next to him and said, "I told Father Boyd that I was mad at you. And he said that for my reconciliation I had to kiss and make up."

"*Did* he now?" Quincy said, looking amazed and then smiling. He winked at her and got up from the pew.

Father Boyd was new enough at St. Joseph's that he did not yet realize he ought to be surprised to see J. Quincy Demarist in the reconciliation room.

"Good evening," the young priest said, "and may Christ's peace be with you."

Quincy thought, *Lord, this guy is just a kid*! He nearly expected the priest's voice to crack any minute.

"Good evening, Father," the penitent replied.

"How can I help you?" Father Boyd asked.

"I was wondering," said Quincy. "That social sin business that you were talking about in your lecture this past week…is that something a person can talk about in confession?"

"Do you want to talk about it?"

"I think so: You might be able to help me," Quincy said, and sighed. "You see, it's been a *long* time since my last confession…."

Miracles Still Happen

(Anointing of the Sick)

The orthopedic ward at Barnes Hospital was the last place Ellie wanted to be. All her life she had exercised, eaten healthy, and even taken calcium pills in recent years to keep her bones strong. But with a broken hip, Ellie now had nowhere else to go.

She had lived alone for the four years since Martin had died, so it would be a while before she could manage on her own again. Friends in her apartment building could help once she got back on her feet. Ellie had brought meals to her neighbor Dolly after her operation, and another neighbor, Johanna, liked to have someone read to her. That was because of the laser treatment she'd gotten for her eyes.

Ellie thought it was strange that the building now seemed to contain mostly old ladies, young couples with different last names on the mailboxes, and women with children but no husbands. *What is the world coming to?* she had often wondered. Still, all the folks in the building managed to live reasonably well together. Ellie liked the children in her building who called her "Grandmaw" — especially Laverne's children, Tyrone and Chanteau. *Who'd ever thought I'd have black grandchildren!* Ellie thought. Ellie didn't have real grandchildren of her own but took her role as "Grandmaw" for Tyrone and Chanteau very seriously. She took it so seriously, in fact, that she had clipped a child's essay from a religious magazine, framed it, and hung it above her bed.

What Is a Grandmother?

A Grandmother is a lady who has no children of her own. She likes other peoples little girls and boys.

Grandmothers don't have to do anything except to be there. There old so they should not play hard or too fast. It is enough if they take us to the store where the pretend horses are, and have a lot of dimes ready. Or if they take us for a walk in the park, they should slow down past things like pretty leaves and caterpillars. They should never say hurry up.

Usually Grandmothers are fat, but not too fat to be able to tie your shoes. They wear glasses and funny underwear. They can take their teeth and gums off.

When Grandmother reads to us, she doesn't skip pages or mind if its the same story over and over again. Everybody should try to have a Grandmother, especially if you don't have television, because they are the only grownups who have lots of time for you.

A nurse walked into Ellie's room and said, "How are you feeling today, Mrs. Cooper?" The nurse drew back the curtains to let in more of the bright February sunlight.

"Oh, OK, I guess," said the patient. Ellie could have kicked herself for going out shopping so late on the day she fell. Once the sun started going down in the winter, she couldn't tell the puddles on the sidewalk from the ice.

"I've told the pastoral-care department that you're here," said the nurse as she straightened out the blanket on the bed. "They like to come around every day, if they can."

"I'm Catholic, you know," Ellie reminded her.

"It's all on the card that your friend filled out for you last night when she brought you in. How's your hip?"

"I guess those calcium pills didn't help after all. They say that women should take more calcium when they get older…to keep their bones strong."

"You never know," the nurse assured her. "It could have been worse if you hadn't taken them. The doctor says the fracture's barely more than a crack."

Well, maybe I did the right thing after all, Ellie thought as she relaxed and closed her eyes again.

❊ ❊ ❊

"Elizabeth Cooper?" a woman's voice called from the doorway.

Ellie opened her eyes and looked toward the woman who stood just inside her door. "Yes?" she said.

"Good morning. My name is Linda Drexel. The nurse said you might like to have a visit from the chaplain today. How are you feeling after your accident?"

"As well as could be expected, I suppose. When do you think the chaplain might be here?"

"I *am* here," said Ms. Drexel, with a smile.

"But I wanted the *Catholic* chaplain," insisted Ellie.

"I *am* the Catholic chaplain." Ms. Drexel smiled.

"But you're a *woman*!" Ellie stated the obvious.

"There are many women in pastoral ministry now. Priests are really busy men these days. But there are a number of priests on call who can come when they're needed, day or night."

"What's the world coming to?" Ellie wondered out loud.

Ms. Drexel moved a chair next to Ellie's bed, and they chatted for a while — about the shortage of priests, changes in the Church…about the freezing weather, and Ellie's hip.

"Would you like to receive the Anointing of the Sick?" Ms. Drexel inquired as she prepared to leave.

"Do you do that too?" asked Ellie, nervously.

"Oh, no," the chaplain reassured her. "That's one thing only priests can do. Not even deacons are allowed to administer that sacrament yet, though I suppose someday they might be."

"But I'm not dying! Is there something that I wasn't told about my condition?" Ellie was getting even more nervous now. "Why should I get Extreme Unction?" she insisted.

Ms. Drexel put the chair back in the corner of the room, then walked back to the bed. "The sacrament is not just for people who are dying. That's why its name was changed to the Anointing of the Sick, to help make that a little clearer."

"When my father died, they didn't call the priest in until just before the end," Ellie said. Her pale forehead wrinkled up with worry.

"That must have been awhile ago."

"It was."

"But you have seen lots of changes in the Church since then; we were just talking about them. The renewal of the Anointing of the Sick must be one of the changes that you just hadn't run across yet."

"I suppose I should be grateful for that. My health has been pretty good, up until now."

"But haven't you been invited to be present when one of your friends was anointed in the hospital or at home?"

"No," said Ellie. "Should I have been?"

"And haven't they had any communal anointing services in your parish?"

"Not that I know of," said Ellie.

"Hmm. I'll have to speak to Father Ambrose about that," said the chaplain.

As the chaplain was leaving, two youngsters bounded into the room, saying, "Hi, Grandmaw! You awake?"

"Tyrone! What are you doing here?" said a surprised Ellie. "And Chanteau! Where's your mother?"

"Right here, Ellie," her neighbor Laverne announced. "Dolly and Johanna asked if I could drive them over to see you, and I thought the kids might like it too."

"Oh, Laverne, thank you," said Ellie. "But I didn't think they allowed children so young to visit people in the hospital."

"I called first," Laverne said, "and they told me on the orthopedic floor it's OK. Besides, if that weren't the case I could have always told the hospital these were yo' grandkids."

"Oh, *Laverne!*" said Ellie, laughing. She waved her hand at Laverne and said, "Go on!"

Two older women entered the room a few seconds later. "Can't keep up with these youngsters the way I used to," said Dolly's loud, husky voice as she entered the room. She panted from the long walk through the hospital halls. "I'm all tuckered out. Guess I better get crackin' on my diet again!"

"How are you, Ellie?" asked Johanna as she came in the room. She walked over to the bed and gave Ellie a little hug.

"Much better now, thanks. My, you look frozen!"

"It's still cold out there, even with the sun shining since this morning," Johanna said. "Not as bad as last night, though, when they brought you in."

"I'm sure glad you were looking out the window when I fell," Ellie said to Laverne. "When I went down I didn't see anyone on the street."

"Your guardian angel was watching out for you," said Dolly confidently.

"I don't know 'bout no *guardian angels*," protested Laverne. "Seems to me that if there were such things, they might have done something more *useful* — like telling Ellie to watch out for the ice on the sidewalk!"

"Oh, dear, what time is it?" asked Ellie, changing the subject.

Johanna lifted her watch right up in front of her own eyes and squinted to see the time. "It's nearly three. Why?"

"The chaplain said that Father Ambrose would be coming by at three to anoint me."

"*Anoint* you! What for?" asked Dolly. "You're not dying!"

"The lady who was here said the priest would explain it. I guess you don't have to be dying to receive the sacrament now. But I wanted to see the priest, and that seemed to be as good a way as any to get him here!"

The ladies chatted for a while, and the children gave Ellie some pictures they had colored for her. Shortly after three a man wearing an olive green shirt and Roman collar walked through the door.

"Hello, Ellie. How are you?" he asked.

Ellie sat up a bit in the bed. She wondered again what the world was coming to with a priest wearing a *green* shirt with his Roman collar. "I'm fine, Father Ambrose. Thanks for coming," she said.

"Dolly, Johanna, nice to see you here too," he added.

"And this here is our neighbor, Laverne Jackson, and her two children, Chanteau and Tyrone," said Dolly.

"Pleased to meet you," said the priest. "I don't think I've met you before."

"I'm not a member of your church, Reverend," explained Laverne. "I'm Pentecostal."

"Wonderful! So you believe in the laying on of hands and praying in the Spirit?"

"Sure, but why do you ask?"

"Because I've come to lay hands on Mrs. Cooper and anoint her. Could you stay and join us?"

"Does that mean us too?" asked Dolly.

"By all means. So often when I visit in the hospital, I have to celebrate the sacrament alone with the patient. I saw Linda Drexel on the way in today, and she tried to remind me of that. It's just that I don't have the time I'd like to have to get in touch with relatives and friends who could join me. But as long as you're all here, you're welcome to stay."

"I didn't know that Catholics believed in healin' by the Holy Spirit," said Laverne.

"Well, we don't call it that, officially. But we do believe that God loves us and wants us to be well, and Catholics have always believed in miraculous cures and healings."

"You mean like at Lourdes and Fatima?" Dolly asked.

"Not only that, but the holy people the Church has canonized as saints have all had miracles attributed to their intercession."

"But we're not saints, Father!" said Johanna with a laugh.

"You don't have to be to pray for someone to be cured. And if the person *is* cured, it's by God's power, not ours."

"How long have you had this in yo' Church?" Laverne asked.

"Well, we Catholics like to think of the Church going all the way back to the time of Christ. In the New Testament you can read how some of the disciples performed miraculous cures, just as Jesus did. Saint James wrote to the Church in Jerusalem that if anyone was sick they should ask the presbyters of the Church to pray over them and anoint them with oil. James said that the people's prayer of faith would help the sick ones and the Lord would raise them up and forgive their sins."

"That doesn't sound like something for dying people," said Ellie.

"You're right," said the priest, turning toward her. "In the early days, anointing was for sick people who wanted to get well. It was not until centuries later that people waited until they were so sick that they were practically dying before they called the priest. That's how the sacrament came to be known as Extreme Unction, or Last Rites."

"Why in the world did they wait so long before asking to be anointed?" Ellie's curiosity was aroused.

"There were a couple of reasons, but the main one seems to have been that as time went on, the sacramental ritual became so elaborate that it could only be performed in a church. People didn't have cars to get around in those days."

"That sounds like a silly reason to me," said Laverne. "The Bible says that the sick person should *send for* the presbyters, not go to church to be anointed."

"When you have a church as old as ours, sometimes you find funny things in its history. At any rate, a few centuries later they changed the ritual so that priests could bring the sacrament out to people again. But by then, everyone had gotten used to the idea that it was mainly for people who were close to dying."

"That's the way it was when I was brought up," commented Ellie.

"We live in a very special century," said the priest, "one of those few in which the Church has seen a great number of changes."

"Just between you and me, Father," said Johanna, "I like the changes. It was always hard for me to follow what was going on at Mass when it was the old way. And now with my eyes being so bad I could never use a missal."

"Well, I don't know what you did in yo' church to change it, but I sure like the results," said Laverne. "My mama say that Catholics always stick to themselves; but me, I know lots of Catholics in the neighborhood."

"Then you should feel right at home with us today," said the priest. "Shall we begin?"

"Wow! Look at that!" said Chanteau, as Father Ambrose took his alb and stole out of the attaché case he had brought with him.

"Hush up, child," whispered her mother. "The reverend is gettin' dressed up for a church service."

"I always like to wear the proper vestments," explained the priest, "but sometimes in emergencies I can't always bring them. Ellie, would you like to receive Communion too?"

"Is that a part of it? I've never been anointed before," she explained.

"It's included in the new rite, so I brought the Blessed Sacrament with me, just in case."

"As long as you're here, Father, you might as well give me the whole works!" Ellie looked pleased now.

"Does that mean you want to go to confession too?"

"Confession? At *my* age, what sins could I commit?"

Father Ambrose took out a crucifix and candle, then set the Hosts and the blessed oil next to them on the bedside table.

"Tyrone, you get back here!" Laverne whispered loudly when

he started making for the table. Obediently, he turned around and stood by his mother again.

"Here are some pamphlets with the sacramental rite in it so everyone can join in," said the priest, passing them around.

"The peace of the Lord be with you," he began.

After the opening prayers and a reading from the Scriptures, Father Ambrose said, "At this point, the rite calls for the laying on of hands. As we all know, Jesus sometimes cured people by touching them, and spiritual healing is sometimes helped when we touch the person who is ill."

He went to the bed and put his hand on Ellie's forehead. Dolly and Johanna went around to the other side and put their hands on their friend's shoulder, while the children went up to the bed and held her hand.

"Reverend," asked Laverne quietly, "in my church we like to touch the part that's in need of healin'. Would it be all right to do that?"

"If Ellie doesn't mind."

Ellie just smiled, and Laverne placed her hand gently on the blanket where her friend's left hip lay.

"Let's pray now for a while," the priest continued, "that the Lord will send healing grace to touch Ellie where she needs it most, in mind and heart, soul and body."

They all prayed in silence except for Laverne, but no one could quite make out her words.

When Laverne had stopped, Father Ambrose lifted his hand from Ellie's forehead, and the others did likewise, taking a step back from the bed.

"It's time for the anointing," he explained. "If you'll follow in the pamphlets with me again." He said the prayers of preparation, and they said the responses.

Then, taking the blessed oil, he anointed Ellie on the forehead and the hands, saying: "Through this holy Anointing, may the Lord in his love and mercy help you with the grace of the Holy Spirit. Amen. May the Lord who frees you from sin save you and raise you up. Amen."

A few more prayers followed, after which Father Ambrose held up the Eucharist where Ellie could see it and said: "This is the Lamb of God who takes away the sins of the world. Happy are those who are called to his supper."

To which Ellie responded: "Lord, I am not worthy to receive you, but only say the word and I shall be healed."

After receiving Communion Ellie closed her eyes for a while. When she opened them again, Father Ambrose said a blessing over her, then blew out the candle.

"That was very nice, Father," said Dolly.

The priest began to put the things he had brought back into the attaché case.

"Thanks for coming, Father," said Ellie, when he walked back to her bed to say good-bye.

"It's my privilege," he responded simply. "It's what I was ordained for."

After he had gone, Ellie motioned Laverne to her bedside and asked, "What was it that you were praying when you touched my hip?"

"We call it praying in the Spirit. Some folks call it praying in tongues. Why?"

"Right there, where you touched me, it sort of felt real warm."

"I guess the reverend was right," said Laverne, squeezing Ellie's hand gently. "You *do* believe in healing by the Holy Spirit!"

❉ ❉ ❉

Holy Name Church was within walking distance of the hospital when the weather was good. Snow fell a few days after Ellie entered the hospital, though, so Linda Drexel drove over to Holy Name instead. The chaplain was not a member of the parish, but since she worked in it, she felt she had a right to speak to the pastor about what was being done (or, rather, *not* being done) for some of its parishioners. In the hospital she had already gotten to know a good number of them personally. She parked her car and walked across the slushy street toward the rectory.

"It's nice of you to come to visit me here," he said, taking her coat at the door. "Usually the only chance we have to sit down and talk is in the hospital cafeteria."

"Someday I'll get an office of my own," Linda said, "but I have a little more wheeling and dealing to do with the hospital administration before *that* happens." She laughed.

"I'll bet I know what's on your mind," Father Ambrose said as he led her into the parlor. "You'd like it if I could have more people present when I administer the Anointing of the Sick — to make it a little more like a communal celebration."

"Well, actually," she said as she sat down in the armchair, "when I thought it over, I figured that I might be able to do that myself. Since I know when you're coming with the sacrament, and since our department has the phone numbers of the patients' nearest friends or relatives, it would be easier for me to do that than you."

"That would be wonderful!" said the priest. "I wonder why no one's ever thought of that before?"

"Sometimes when a new person comes into a place they can see new possibilities that have been overlooked by the staff who have been working there for a while," explained the young chaplain.

"True enough," Father Ambrose commented. "Is that why you're here then?"

"Well, actually," Linda went on, "I *have* come to ask a favor, only a different one. I've gotten to know a number of your elderly parishioners, and I've noticed that many of them are not aware of the full meaning of the Anointing of the Sick."

"I've noticed that too," admitted the pastor. "I find myself explaining it over and over again every time I bring the sacrament to people."

"I hope you won't feel that this is infringing too much on your turf," said the young woman, "but I was wondering if you'd consider a communal anointing service in the parish. It would give you an opportunity to explain the meaning of the sacrament to many people at the same time."

"As a matter of fact, I've thought of it a number of times. But every time I try to get around to it, something seems to come up — usually a call from the hospital!"

"I suspected as much," said Linda with a gleam of insight in her eyes. "An anointing service could reach a number of people who might not otherwise call you individually because even though they're sick they know they probably aren't going to die. You could explain the sacrament and anoint them all at once."

"Good idea." Father Ambrose stroked his beard. "I thought of something else, as well: The spiritual and physical benefits of the sacrament might even help some people to feel better so they wouldn't need an individual anointing."

"Yes," said Linda. "The more I learn about gerontology, the more I'm thinking that many people, especially older ones, have health problems that are related to their not being touched. When people get older they tend to live alone and get emotionally isolated. I'm always amazed at how much better my patients feel if they let me hold their hand while I'm talking with them. And after they get to know me, they let me hug them...."

"You're not suggesting that we introduce hugs into the sacramental ritual, I hope!" the priest interrupted.

"Oh, no. But I was thinking that you might connect it to a social event. If you had the sacramental ceremony just before noon, say, you could follow it with a lunch in the church basement. Then people would have even more of a chance to shake hands and exchange hugs, all of which would be good for their emotional and spiritual well-being."

"All well and good," said Father Ambrose. "But just who is supposed to get all this going? I don't have the time!"

"Well, actually, I've thought about that too. Why not get the people to do it for themselves? They have much more time than either you or I do. It'll keep them too busy to be lonely. Some of them, I'm sure, are lectors, ushers, and Eucharistic ministers who already have some familiarity with parish liturgies...."

"Excuse me for interrupting again. But speaking of liturgies, you know we *could* celebrate the sacrament within the context of a Mass."

"Well, actually, I was hoping that you'd say that too."

"A Mass on a weekday or Saturday morning. Which do you think would be better?"

"Why don't we ask the people who'll be planning it and let them decide?"

"Followed by a lunch. But who would organize that?"

"You forget, Father, we have some tremendous cooks in the parish, like all the men and women who put on the annual barbecue in September! I'm sure that many of them would be delighted to cook for more than just one person for a change. So...could they use the kitchen in the church basement?"

"Oh, sure, that goes without saying!" said Father.

❊   ❊   ❊

Weeks later the snow had melted, and Ellie's hip was feeling much better. Her release from the hospital set a new record, she was told, and she was proud of that. The doctors examining her x-rays said that her hip was mending faster than they had ever seen before. When she asked them what they thought the reason was, they confessed they didn't know for sure. Ellie had a good idea what did it, but at this point she didn't think about it much. She was just happy to be out of the hospital and back in her familiar surroundings again.

"Today's the day I'll put the hospital walker in the closet for good," she said aloud to herself one Sunday morning as she made coffee. The cane would be much more dignified, she knew. She could even make it around without the cane at home. She reasoned that it was safer, though, to wait until summer before trying to walk outside without extra support for her leg. No sense courting trouble needlessly.

The phone rang with a call from Johanna, her upstairs neighbor. "Ellie? Do you feel well enough to walk, or should I call a cab for the three of us?"

"I think I can keep up with Dolly," answered Ellie, "and the exercise will be good for both of us. Better tell her to hurry up though. I hate being late for Mass."

❊   ❊   ❊

Although Holy Name wasn't her home parish, Linda Drexel sat in one of the church's back pews this Sunday morning. She wanted to get a feel for the congregation in order to help Father Ambrose with the anointing service. As she watched a trio of elderly women return to their seats after Communion, Linda spotted Ellie. It was then that the chaplain *knew* Ellie was the right person to organize an anointing service for older folks in the parish.

"She's naturally outgoing and independent and can act on her own initiative," Linda whispered to Father Ambrose after Mass. "She also knows how to plan a healthy menu, and she's even taking an exercise class for seniors. I think someone like that could be ideal for arranging the luncheon after the anointing service."

"Go for it!" Father Ambrose told Linda. "Catch her before she whizzes out of here."

When Linda approached Ellie with the idea, Ellie said, "Don't ask me to plan any liturgy though. I don't know anything about that sort of thing! I know who you *could* ask though."

With Ellie's help, Linda assembled a liturgy team to assist Father

Ambrose in planning the first Mass of Anointing for the elderly in the parish.

One of the first decisions of the liturgy planning team was to set the date of the Mass for the third Thursday of the month. They reasoned that it was the five days between the weekends that most retired persons found the hardest to fill; therefore a weekday Mass would be best.

The parish secretary got behind the new developments by writing stories about the seniors' club in the parish bulletin. The bulletin announcements made it clear that Anointing of the Sick was not just for emergency illnesses.

Father Ambrose helped the parish prepare for the event by finding ways to mention the sacrament in his weekend homilies, no matter what text he was preaching on. He wanted to make sure everyone understood that people with chronic illnesses could also be helped by prayer, anointing, and the laying on of hands. For those who still thought the sacrament was primarily for people who were dying, Father Ambrose suggested that once people were over sixty-five, they were close enough to dying that they could certainly join in the communal anointing liturgy.

Ellie started getting things going by making phone calls. *How many to prepare for?* Ellie wondered. She, Father Ambrose, and Linda Drexel guessed somewhere around fifty. Nobody was absolutely certain, but they rationalized that if they were *all* wrong they could console one another.

As planned, Ellie, Dolly, and Johanna were the first ones to arrive a little before ten. At ten o'clock the first work crew came: people to staff the kitchen, a group of sturdy men to set up the tables and chairs. At ten-thirty, a second group came to help set out silverware and dishes, while the liturgy team upstairs opened the church doors and turned on the lights. At quarter to eleven Ellie could tell from the sound of the creaking floor overhead that the first parishioners were arriving.

"Time for Mass!" she announced. She set the ovens on low and the work crew headed upstairs. Before Ellie closed the door to the cafeteria she glanced around the room one last time, satisfied that everything was in place.

And it was — for fifty people, more or less. But then Ellie made it up the stairs and looked into the church. "My word, *look* at all those people!" she said to no one in particular.

There must be at least a hundred of them, she figured. Looking around, she saw the twenty-five or so that she personally knew were coming. The parish secretary had given her a list of others who had expressed an interest — about another twenty-five. But who were all these others?

Suddenly it dawned on her. The other people were not old, like the ones she had been expecting to see. Some were middle-aged, some were young, some were even children. Some came in wheelchairs, some wore casts, some used crutches. And, of course, some were not elderly or sick at all. They just wanted to be there — to pray with and for the others.

Fortunately, the pastor was still in the vestibule, where he had been greeting all the people coming in. From the somewhat dazed look on his smiling face, Ellie guessed that he was as surprised at the turnout as she was.

"Father Ambrose!" she called, walking toward him. "What are we going to *do* with all these people?"

"We're going to pray over the ones who want to be prayed over and anoint the ones who want to be anointed, of course! The liturgy will take a little longer, but we'll manage. Jesus said that we should go out and invite the sick and the blind and the lame, and from the looks of things he knew what he was talking about!"

Looking past the priest, Ellie spotted Linda Drexel, who was just arriving from the hospital. "Linda! Come look! There must be a hundred people here!" she called out.

"A hundred?" asked Linda, running up the front entrance steps. "We were only counting on fifty!"

"I know, but we forgot about the others."

"What others?"

"The people who aren't elderly and ill but just sick or hurt...and the people who brought them...and the ones who just came to be here with them."

"Well, actually," said the young chaplain, "that's one thing that I *hadn't* thought of! What are we going to do?"

"Father Ambrose says that he can take care of them for the liturgical part, but how are we going to *feed* them all? The announcement in the church bulletin said that everyone was invited for a hot lunch afterward. But we don't have enough food for all these people!"

"Hmm. Do you have enough plates and silverware and things?"

"Well, sure, there are lots in the cupboards that we haven't touched."

"And does it have to be a *hot* lunch?" The wheels in Linda's mind seemed to be turning.

"What are you driving at?"

"Well, actually, I'm thinking more of driving *to* the hospital and back. The head of the cafeteria food service is a friend of mine, and I'm hoping he'll let us have some food for sandwiches and salad for…how many did you say? Fifty people?"

"But won't he get in trouble if he does that?" asked Ellie, worried.

"You never know until you ask," said Linda, heading back toward her car. "Pray for a miracle!"

Ellie turned around and saw that the vestibule was empty. Father Ambrose had already started down the aisle to begin the Mass for twice as many people as they had expected. That was a miracle in itself, Ellie figured.

As she walked down the aisle herself, looking for where Dolly and Johanna were sitting, she realized that in all the excitement she had left her cane downstairs. Touching her hand to her hip, she counted another miracle. *And if two, why not three?* she wondered, *or even more?*

What *was* it about this Mass that was different, Ellie asked herself. She couldn't see it, but she could sense it somehow. Not until the people in the pews sat down for the first reading could she see what it was. Unlike at most Masses, the people filled the first few rows instead of the back ones. *Not at all like Sunday morning,* she thought. The people in wheelchairs sat in the aisles. *You hardly ever see those on Sunday. How'd they ever get those wheelchairs up the front steps, anyway? Another miracle!* she thought.

The first reading from 1 Corinthians 1:18-25 spoke of God's power to save, and how divine weakness is stronger than human strength.

It's comforting to know, Ellie reflected, *that where my strength leaves off, God's is just beginning!* The Gospel reading from Mark 2:1-12 was the story of the paralyzed man whose friends brought him to Jesus; and before Jesus cured him, he forgave his sins.

In his homily, Father Ambrose used both readings to teach the congregation about the two dimensions of God's healing in the sacrament of Anointing of the Sick: "It's so good to see you all here today! No one is more surprised, or more pleased, than I am to see how many of you have come to the first liturgy of communal anointing here at Holy Name. Yet I realized even before the Mass began that I should not be surprised. If we look in the Gospels, there are literally dozens of stories like the one we just heard about people coming to Jesus to be healed. It sometimes seems that whenever Jesus wasn't preaching, he was healing people.

"I realize, then, that you have come to be healed. And I can assure you that each of you will be. How can I be so sure of that? Because Saint Paul reminds us in the first reading that God's power is more than ours, and that God wants to use that power to save us. Saint Mark also reminds us in the second reading that God's power to heal is not only physical but also spiritual.

"People sometimes wonder why so many times when people asked Jesus to cure their bodies, he also forgave their sins. It's because to the Jewish mind — and Jesus was born Jewish, remember — evil was something both physical and spiritual. We can see this in our own lives. When we are physically sick or hurting, we are often emotionally down and psychologically depressed. Our soul is sick when our body is hurting. On the other hand, when we're really happy we can forget that we have a fever or the pain that was bothering us goes away.

"Doctors and psychologists tell us more and more these days that our body and spirit are closely connected. Jesus, however, already knew this two thousand years ago! When he reached out to people, he wanted to heal them spiritually as well as physically. In the sacrament of the Anointing of the Sick, Christ extends this same twofold healing power to us. God wants us to be completely healed. We need only to open ourselves up to the saving power of God's grace to begin to experience that healing.

"What kind of healing will we receive from God, then, if we come to the sacrament and ask God to save us? Before it happens, we don't actually know. God knows better than we do what we really need. What we have to do is to trust that God will extend to us the healing power that we most need at this moment.

"I have sometimes seen people get physically better after receiving the Anointing of the Sick. When that happens, I am truly thankful to God. But I have almost always seen people get spiritually better after being anointed. They are more at peace with God and more united to God's will for them, whatever it might be. I am just as thankful when I see that happen.

"In a short while we will put our hands on those of you who are not completely healthy, and we will pray over you silently, each in our own way. Then I will anoint you with the sacrament, and I will pray the prayer of the Church for your healing in both body and soul.

"Let us pray, therefore, that those who come to the sacrament today will receive God's healing power in the very way that they need it most."

Father Ambrose then led a short litany of prayers for healing which had been prepared by the liturgy team, and everyone prayed the responses that they found in their Mass booklets. After that he invited all those who wished to receive the sacrament to come forward for the laying on of hands. He also suggested that anyone who wanted to join him in praying for their relatives and friends should come forward as well.

"Even *I* know how to do that," Ellie whispered to Dolly. But then a puzzled look came over her face, as if she were trying to decide what to do. A look of resolution wiped it away as she made her way through the crowded aisle and up to the space in front of the front pew where Father Ambrose was about to begin the laying on of hands.

"Father," she asked before he could say anything, "are you allowed to do both?"

"I'm sorry, Ellie, I don't follow you," said the pastor, taken aback. "Both what?"

"Can you both pray for somebody else and then have people pray over you? In the same ceremony, I mean?"

"To tell you the truth, I never thought of that," said Father Ambrose. "But I don't see why not."

Father Ambrose laid his hands on the first parishioner's head while her friends joined him in prayer by touching her shoulder.

Ellie hurried back to Johanna. "Father says it's all right," Ellie announced.

"What's all right?"

"We can go up together, and when he prays over me, you can too, just like you did in the hospital. And then when it's your turn, I'll pray over you!"

"And Dolly can pray for both of us," suggested Johanna.

"Don't you want to be prayed over too?" Ellie turned to Dolly.

"I'm not sure that being a little overweight makes me a candidate for that!" said her friend with a smile. "Besides, with you two, I have my hands full. Maybe some other time. I'm not *that* old, you know!"

When the trio saw that there was some space in front of the first pew, they walked to where they could hear the priest. Before he laid his hands in prayer on each of his parishioners, he asked them what had brought them to the healing service and talked with them briefly about how they were feeling.

That Father Ambrose is such a nice man to add a personal touch to the ceremony like that, thought Ellie. Suddenly a light went on in Ellie's head. *I wonder if he's doing that to give Linda some extra time to find something for our lunch? I'll bet that's it! That Father Ambrose sure is sharp!*

When the pastor reached Johanna, he asked her how her eyes were doing and if there was anything else she would like him to pray for.

"Well, my diabetes has been giving me some trouble lately, and that's what's *really* causing me the eye problems."

"If your friends, then, will join me," said the priest, "let's ask the Lord to touch you where you most need to be healed."

Ellie and Dolly put their hands on their friend's shoulder, and the three prayed silently for a few moments over her.

Laverne should see me now! thought Ellie, as they finished praying for Johanna. *She'd think I was becoming Pentecostal!*

Now it was Ellie's turn. She again opened her heart to whatever healing God might want to give her. But unlike in the hospital, she did not feel anything physical this time. But she did feel inner peace. She *had* felt that when Father Ambrose had anointed her a few weeks earlier.

When the laying on of hands was finished, Father Ambrose added something to the ceremony that Ellie had not seen before. In the hospital, the priest had brought blessed oil with him. But here in church he said a prayer of blessing over the oil that he was about to use for the sacramental anointing. Then once again the pastor asked those who wished to be anointed to come forward for the sacrament. While she waited her turn, Ellie realized that she had never really given much thought to the significance of oil before.

When you have a burn or dry skin, oil or cream really helps to take the hurt away, she pondered. *This anointing, too, seems to be taking some of the hurt away.* She could see it in the calm faces and relaxed shoulders of the people the priest touched. And as he prayed the Prayer of Anointing again and again for each person, she sensed a spiritual peace descending on all those who were gathered there — like oil cascading onto parched leather to make it smooth and supple. As the Mass was ending, Ellie suddenly realized that she had forgotten all about lunch and the impending crisis. "Come on," she whispered to Dolly and Johanna. "We'd better go downstairs and set the food out on the serving tables."

"What there is of it," said Dolly. "I hope people aren't too disappointed."

"We'll make it stretch somehow," was Ellie's confident reply.

Ellie herself wasn't sure how or why. Was it confidence in her own ability to manage in a crisis? Was it her growing trust in Linda Drexel's talents? Or was it a deeper faith in God — a belief in miracles?

"Linda, you did it!" cried Ellie, as soon as she saw the shopping bags. "The cafeteria manager let you have the food after all."

"Well, actually, he didn't," admitted Linda, "but he sent me to a food wholesaler that he deals with, and he let me use his account number on the purchase order since I didn't have any money. He turned out to be the right person to ask after all. But we still have to pay him back before the end of the month."

"What did you bring with you?" asked Johanna as she started emptying out the bags.

"Bread — white, rye, and whole wheat; cold cuts and cheese; cafeteria packets of mustard and mayonnaise; and a few quarts of coleslaw, potato salad, and macaroni salad. Plus there's some lettuce and tomatoes. He said it should feed forty to sixty."

"It's more than enough," Ellie assured her. "We old folks don't eat as much as you youngsters!"

"But don't forget," reminded Dolly, "we're not just having senior citizens for lunch today. Too bad we couldn't have a hot meal for everyone, like we wanted to."

"It's not how warm the food is that's important," replied Linda. "It's how warm the company is. I think everyone's going to feel real cozy."

"Cozy isn't the word," said Ellie sharply. "*Crowded* is more like it, unless we get some more tables and chairs set up. Linda could you take charge of that?"

"Sure, I'll have the men help me as soon as they come down."

"But how are we going to pay for it all?" asked Dolly.

"I think we'll manage," assured Ellie. "We were going to set out some baskets for donations anyway. With twice as many people here as we expected, we should be able to collect more than we were counting on to cover just the hot food."

"Ellie, you think of everything!" said her friend in amazement.

"Speaking of everything, we still have to get everything out of the ovens," Ellie remembered out loud. "Hear the floor squeaking? That means they'll be down in a few minutes!"

The three women uncovered the hot dishes on one serving table and the sandwich fixings on another. The first people walked in the door and Linda recruited them to help set up chairs. The set-up team put out more dishes and silverware. Despite the unexpected activity, everyone worked smoothly together.

Ellie stood aside and surveyed the scene. "Now have I forgotten anything?" she mused aloud. Then she saw it — propped against the wall in a corner was her cane.

Yes! she thought, and smiled. *Don't need things to lean on when you have people for support. Makes you sort of believe in miracles — even expect them.*

Like a Horse and Carriage

(Matrimony)

"I don't see why we have to take *marriage* lessons." The anger in Bob's voice underlined every evenly spaced syllable as he drove down the country road.

"Please don't bring that up again," pleaded Janet, "especially now when we're on our way to the weekend."

They had been through this a dozen times before. Each time she had tried to explain why they could not get married in her home parish unless they agreed to participate in the Marriage Discovery program. Marriage Discovery was a weekend retreat for engaged couples that the diocesan marriage and family ministry office sponsored. They could have instead participated in a one-night-a-week style series of discussions at Janet's parish, but with Bob constantly working late on weeknights it just hadn't been possible.

"After all, we're not teenagers," said Bob. "I could see it if we hadn't been to college or hadn't known each other for a couple of years already. We've saved up enough money to get a good start in life, and you can't say we don't know anything about sex."

Janet knew that the former pastor from her parish was now stationed at the retreat center. Hoping that the subject would not come up in front of him, Janet kept her uneasy silence.

"If you wanted a church wedding," said Bob, "I'm sure we could have found a minister to do one with less fuss."

Why was it, Janet wondered, that she and Bob seemed to get along so peacefully, but when it came to certain subjects they ran into a brick wall? She assured herself that she was no religious fanatic, but she did feel strongly about getting married in the parish where she had grown up. Her parents and friends still lived there, and it held many happy memories for her. How many times had she looked up at the altar and seen herself standing there in a wedding dress? Even though Bob was a nonpracticing Catholic, she had assumed that he would understand her feelings about wanting to marry in St. Theresa's. On this subject and some others, though, it almost seemed as though Bob couldn't hear her.

Lost in her private thoughts, she barely noticed when they drove up the long driveway of the Ave Maria Retreat Center.

※　※　※

"Welcome!" said Father Benson, as Janet and Bob entered the room where the first talk of the Friday evening session would soon start. "Janet, it's so good to see you after all this time! And this must be Bob," he said, extending his hand. "I've heard so much about you from Janet's parents."

"A few good things along with all the others, I hope," said Bob, smiling.

"Positively," assured the priest she wanted to impress. Janet breathed a sigh of relief when she saw her fiancé trying to be gracious, even humorous.

"Come on in and meet the others in the group," Father Benson said. The marriage preparation group was not as large as Janet had expected. Perhaps it was because not that many couples planned January weddings.

The others made the rounds of introducing themselves. Only one couple could be classified as "teenagers" — Dave and Kathy had just graduated from high school. Kathy had gotten a job as a salesclerk, and Dave had recently enrolled in a training program for servicing business computers. They planned to be married soon after Dave got his first placement with his new company.

"The honeymoon will just have to wait until I've earned some vacation time," said Dave, "but we'll be happy just to be married."

The second couple looked as though they might be in their late thirties. Paula had been married before, and the divorce had left her struggling with three teenagers to feed. This was the first time for Ray though. At first, Ray had been dubious about surrendering his bachelor life, but the more he got to know Paula, the more attractive the idea became.

"I knew that I could never take the place of their real father," said Ray, "but over the months her kids came to accept me as a friend, and that sort of cinched it," Ray explained. "I found that I was spending so much time at Paula's house that it didn't make sense to live alone anymore."

Father Benson introduced the third couple as the lay coordinators of the group — which took Bob and Janet a little by surprise.

"I thought that you would be leading these sessions, Father," said Janet.

"Liz and Al are very special people, and I'm sure that by the time the program's over you'll be glad you had them in your group," said Father Benson with evident pride. "There's no way that I could head up all the marriage preparation groups that we've got going in the diocese. We hold one of these weekends every month, so that's twelve in all. Sometimes the groups that are aiming at summer weddings get too big, so we divide them since we like to keep the groups small and informal. Liz and Al will be with you for the whole program, and I'll be joining you from time to time when you need me to be here. Right now, though, I'll turn the meeting over to them and I'll just take a seat over here on the side."

After glancing at his wife to check out which of them should start, Al began. "Our purpose this first evening of the weekend is just to get acquainted and to let you know what we'll be doing during the weekend. We'll get to our schedule a little later on, so at this point we'd just like to tell you a little more about ourselves.

"Liz and I have been married for eleven years now. We have three children, and we've been active in this marriage preparation program for a little over two years. We're not marriage counselors by any means, but between our own experience as a couple, as parents, and as participants in this program we hope that we'll be able to answer most of your questions, or at least be able to tell you how to find the answers.

"Speaking of questions, are there any that you'd like to ask right now?"

Bob jumped right in. "One thing I don't understand is why we are here at all. I don't really like the idea of any church telling me when I can or can't get married."

Janet moved uncomfortably in her chair while her fiancé spoke. One of the other women extended a reassuring glance to her.

"The reason I asked for questions is because that's one that many people have, not just you, Bob," said Al. "It's good to get it out on the floor right at the beginning. What you're asking is a Church policy question, and it's good to answer it while Father Benson is here with us."

"Thanks, Al, and thank you, Bob, for bringing it up," the priest began. "The Church has always been concerned that Catholics should enter marriages that are happy and enduring. In the early days the Church fought to uphold the ideal of Christian marriage against the pagan notions that prevailed in the Roman Empire. When the Empire collapsed, there was no one to protect the rights of people who might be taken advantage of by being forced to marry against their will or who might be deserted or orphaned. That's when the Church introduced its own laws regulating marriage, including rules for separation and inheritance. Today, however, the Church is moving away from the legalistic approach to marriage that it inherited from the Middle Ages and is instead turning toward a more pastoral approach."

"What does *pastoral* mean?" asked Bob.

"It means that we're trying to be helpful, not just laying down the law to people," replied the priest.

"But Janet said we couldn't get married without coming to these classes first," insisted Bob. "That sounds like laying down the law to me."

"If you wanted to go your own way, of course," the priest said, "the Church could not prevent that. Anyone can get married these days just by going to city hall. But if you're interested in a Christian marriage, or what we call a *sacramental* marriage, then the Church wants to do everything it can to help you get started on the right foot."

"I know a little about sacraments, but I really don't know much," Bob confessed. "So sacramental marriage sounds sort of mysterious to me."

"In a way, it is," said Father Benson. "It's just as mysterious as human love, caring, commitment, dedication, healing, and forgiveness. As Catholics, though, we believe that these human realities are also signs that point beyond themselves to God. In the case of marriage, we believe that the relationship between husband and wife is a sign of the relationship between Christ and the Church. To be that kind of sign requires a special kind of relationship."

"It sounds so…so *universal*," said Bob. "Like responsibility for the whole *galaxy* will rest on our shoulders!"

Liz broke in, saying, "You make it sound so ponderous…and difficult!"

"Now you see, Bob," said the priest sitting back in his chair, "why we ask laypeople to be in this program — to translate the theology into English! How would you say it, Liz?"

"I'd just say that the kind of love that should be present in a sacramental marriage is the same kind of love that God has for us. God is generous and caring and forgiving. God never gives up on us, always wants the best for us, and never walks away from loving us, even when we're difficult.

"You don't always see that kind of love in the world, but when you do, something inside you tells you that's the way love ought to be. You don't see it in two youngsters making eyes at each other or in two actors who have the hots for one another on the screen. You see it in a husband who takes care of his wife when she's sick, in a wife who goes back to work because the family needs it to make ends meet, in a man who believes that his wife is more important than his career, in an old couple who say they owe the best years of their lives to each other. It's a kind of love that lasts, that gets better year after year, that grows through two people giving themselves completely to each other. That's the kind of relationship I think of when I try to imagine how God loves us, and how we ought to love God."

"You really said it well," said Father Benson.

"And the beauty of it," Liz continued, "is that it's the happiest kind of love there is. It's the most joyful and the most rewarding. Sometimes it looks like you have to give up a lot, but in the end you find that you have everything you ever wanted."

"Coming back down to earth," said Al as he put his hand on his wife's, "you could say that the purpose of this weekend is to help you get a better handle on what the Church wants every marriage to be like and to give you a shove in the right direction!"

Bob laughed a little at the way Al put it. Janet found herself thinking that maybe she was more like Bob than she realized. She hadn't really understood what she had gotten them involved in.

Al picked up a handful of information packets and passed them around. "Now, if there aren't any more questions I'll move on to the next step here."

Papers rustled as the packets made the rounds.

"The whole weekend is explained in this first set of stapled sheets," said Al."

"Once you finish looking at the schedule we'd like you to fill out a questionnaire," added Liz. "There's a separate one for each of you in the packets. Please answer them without consulting each other. After you've filled them out, though, feel free to talk about what you've written. The questionnaire's main purpose is to act as a discussion starter, both between couples and with the whole group when we meet again tomorrow morning after breakfast."

❋   ❋   ❋

"Just what I need, more paperwork," said Bob. "I thought I could use some of the spare time for catching up on office work."

"Oh, *Bob*, is that all you can say? I think the first session was quite nice," said Janet as they strolled down one of the halls at the retreat center. The high vaulted ceiling hovered over them as their sneakers occasionally squeaked on the waxed tile floor. Outdoors, crickets chirped. An owl hooted.

"This place kind of gives me the creeps," said Bob. "You'd think a place to learn about marriage would be a little more, well, *homey*."

"It used to be a seminary," said Janet.

Bob looked up at the dim schoolhouse-style light suspended from a chain above them. "No wonder there's a priest shortage. I could never stand learning how to be a priest way out here in the middle of nowhere."

"But people come here for peace and prayer and quiet conversation. It's not supposed to be like our dorms were in college."

They clasped each other's hands and walked a little further in silence. Bob stopped and put his arms around Janet's waist. "Well...your room or mine?"

Janet thought a moment before answering. "Bob, you'll sleep in your room and I'll sleep in mine."

Bob complained, "Come on, Janet!"

Janet sighed and then spoke again, "We'll be together next weekend. Now, why don't we work on this questionnaire so we're ready when we meet with the group again?"

❋   ❋   ❋

"Papers, papers, papers…" said Bob. "This looks like a lot of work to me."

"Well, let's give it a try, at least," said Janet.

Bob snuggled up to her on the couch in one of the building's lounges.

"I've read through all of this. It's pretty interesting," said Janet.

"More interesting than me?" said Bob as he kissed her neck.

"Interesting in a different sort of way. Why don't you get started on it and see for yourself. I'm going to start on mine." Bob rolled his eyes in exasperation.

"It doesn't take that long. By the time you're done I'll be finished, and we can talk about it."

"But what about dessert?" he said, holding her close again. "We forgot dessert tonight."

"Oh, Bob, there's lots of time for that some other day. But we're supposed to be getting married in only six months!" The desperation in her expression made her voice squeak. Bob did not pick up on her seriousness. He seemed to think she was just being stubborn. Rather than fight it, he picked up the questionnaire and started reading it. Janet began filling in her answers.

After ten minutes Janet asked, "Learn anything?"

"Huh?"

"From doing the questionnaire," she said.

"What's there to learn? It doesn't tell you anything. It just asks questions about everything under the sun — your family background, your parents' attitudes, your own ideas about money and budgeting, sex and birth control, religion, raising children, the kind of wedding you want, what you expect of your marriage partner, and a whole bunch of other things. I thought I had finished taking exams in college."

"So, what did you put down?"

"Me? I didn't put down anything. If the subject comes up at the group tomorrow I'll just wing it like I do at the office."

"But I want to learn about *you* — about how you feel about all these things," Janet persisted.

"So what do you want to know? I'll tell you. My family background? You've already met my folks. Their attitudes? Strictly middle class. Money? That's why we've postponed the marriage as long as we have. My ideas on sex? We've been through all that before. Religion? I'm neither pro nor con. Children? One girl and one boy, but only after we're settled. The wedding? I'll let you arrange that."

"And what do you expect of me, your future marriage partner?"

"Well..." said Bob. He held her waist and snuggled up.

"Oh, Bob, be serious," protested Janet.

"I *am* being serious," Bob insisted. "But I refuse to beat the subject to death, the way this program you got us into wants us to. Life's too short for that."

"Well, what about the questions about your childhood? You've never told me much about that, and I really want to know you better. That shouldn't be too hard, and we've got the time."

Bob finally took the hint and talked about his boyhood. He talked about his brother and two sisters. "Yeah Ed and I used to scare our sisters...." He spoke about the old neighborhood. "Jimmy Schumacher and me used to ride our bikes and pop wheelies over the dirt hills at the end of the street. We accidentally busted a window once and...."

Bob seemed proud of his boyhood antics. He enjoyed recalling his past. When he talked about the jobs that he'd had and the plans he had built for his future, Janet realized that she had similar experiences and that they both had similar dreams about many things. They had grown up so much alike, even though they had never known each other until two years ago. She felt closer to him than she had in a long while.

"Wow, I didn't know I could talk like that," said Bob, glancing at his watch.

"Don't forget the other part though."

"What other part?"

"The directions say that each partner in the dialogue needs to do what the other did," Janet reminded him.

"So?"

"So now it's your turn to ask me about my childhood. Or don't you want to know?"

"Of course, I do," said Bob, playing along.

Janet didn't talk so much about the things that had happened to her as she was growing up but about how she felt about them. She didn't plan it that way, but it came out that way. They had a different way of perceiving the same sorts of events. She'd get engrossed in talking about her sisters, about how much she hated high school, about some boys that she had dated who were creeps.

Janet watched Bob as she talked and noticed that he seemed to be really interested. The look in his eyes made her want to open up to him even more.

"You know, I never really understood a lot of things about you," said Bob, "but what you were saying a while ago made some pieces fall into place."

"Like what?"

"Like the way you talked about your sisters, for example. I think that one of the reasons we get into arguments is because you didn't grow up with boys, and the boys you did meet in school were obviously wimps. I see now that when we're talking sometimes you're not getting my drift."

"Am I getting your drift tonight?"

"Beautifully, baby. Want to take a little break now?"

"Uh-huh," she said, moving closer to him on the couch.

❄ ❄ ❄

Right after breakfast Al addressed the entire group in the dining room. "Did everyone do their homework?" he asked. The twinkle in his eye betrayed the false seriousness of his voice.

Janet was relieved to discover that none of the couples had actually completed the entire questionnaire, although all of them had started it. They spread the papers on the table in front of them as they got ready to get into the meeting.

"It sure is nice having *real* married people here," Kathy said to Al's wife, Liz. "It's nice that you volunteer your time to help engaged couples like us."

"Why, thank you, Kathy," Liz returned. "We'll start here in the dining room today since we have so many papers, otherwise we would meet in the lecture room."

"Our meetings really ought to be informal," Al picked up. "Not like school classes but more like adult discussion. Personally, I like a lot of give-and-take."

"You mean you don't have an agenda for the discussion?" asked Bob, not sure whether he should be puzzled or irritated.

"I can see that you're a man who doesn't like to waste time." Al had caught the tone in Bob's voice. "Don't worry, we'll always have a lot to do! Sometimes Liz or I will lead, but right now we'll let you folks set the agenda. Why don't you start us off, Bob? You can pick any topic on the questionnaire."

Bob flipped through the blank pages in front of him, looking for something familiar. "As a matter of fact," he said, "the topic that interests me most isn't here, but it's one that Janet and I have talked about." He almost added, *often,* but he realized that Janet would know that wasn't true.

"And what's that?"

"It has to do with raising our...family. I've heard that non-Catholics have to swear in writing to bring up the family in the Catholic religion."

"You must have heard that quite awhile ago!" Al raised his eyebrows. "In reality, all that was asked twenty or thirty years ago was a verbal promise. We still think that religion is important for children, but today the Church just asks that the non-Catholic allow the Catholic to practice his or her faith. Of course, the Church prefers that the children be raised Catholic, but now that almost half the marriages in our country are interfaith marriages we realize that making a stronger demand might do more harm than good."

"Such as?" Bob pressed him.

"Such as discouraging some people from even considering marrying a Catholic. Or such as making Catholics choose between their religion and the person they love. The Church does not want to force people out of a Catholic marriage, it wants to invite them into one."

"Speaking about Catholic marriage," Ray broke in, "you may have to update me on something that came up when Paula and I were doing the questionnaire. When I was in Catholic school the catechism said that children were the main purpose of marriage. Being just a kid, that seemed fine at the time, but I can't say that that's the reason I want to marry Paula. Not that we've excluded the possibility of having children of our own, but right now it looks as though her three are as much as we can handle."

"Both emotionally and financially," Paula added, "having another child would be a big strain on our marriage. I'd have to quit work at least for a while."

"And I'm wondering," Ray went on, "whether I should try to be a daddy at my age. I'm forty-five, you see. But I know that the Church has some strong opinions about birth control, and especially about getting married with the idea of not having children. Would the Church say that we could not get married if we didn't have any more kids?"

Al said, "That's a good question, Ray. In fact, it's two or three questions, if I'm hearing you right. One of them is whether the Church says that you have to have children, and the simple answer to that is no, you don't. Sometimes people get married knowing that they can't have children of their own, but the Church still blesses their marriage.

"The other questions that I hear you asking have to do with birth control. One is whether the Catholic Church is against birth control, and the answer to that question is no, despite what many people think. What the Church disapproves of is certain forms of birth control that are not natural, but the Church is one hundred percent behind natural family planning. Later on a couple from the diocesan natural family planning office will explain more about NFP. You should realize, too, that many Catholics in good conscience and even some theologians don't believe that modern birth control methods are against God's law. This doesn't mean that they are bad Catholics, though.

"Whether a Catholic couple in good conscience could practice birth control with the intention of never having children is something else again. The Church believes that a couple who are so self-centered that they would never be willing to share their life with children would not be entering a truly Christian marriage. The key issue here is selfishness and not being open to new life. It doesn't seem to me from what you've said, though, that you've completely closed off that possibility."

"You're right," said Ray thoughtfully, "we're just not sure at this point what would be the best thing to do."

"Then it seems to me that this is something that you and Paula will have to pray about and seek some advice about, to discern what God wants you to do. How does that sound to you, Paula?"

"I'm just so glad that Ray is the kind of man that I can do that with," said Paula softly. "He's just so different from my first husband, and I thank God every day for this second chance. My first husband saw himself as a very law-abiding Catholic, but a lot of times I think he used that as an excuse to cut off discussion. It was his decision, not mine, to have children right away. I love my kids, but I just wish we could have talked about it sometimes — that and other things."

No one seemed to know what to say next, so Janet asked, "Is that why your marriage didn't work out? I don't mean to pry, but I noticed that a good part of the questionnaire was about communicating with the person you intend to marry."

"I don't mind your asking, Janet. I'm glad to share what I learned the hard way. If Hank and I would have had the benefit of learning about the importance of communication in a program like this one, maybe we wouldn't have made the mistake that we did."

"You feel your first marriage was a mistake?" asked Janet.

"That's my understanding of what an annulment means," said Paula simply. "It means we shouldn't have gotten married in the first place."

"But why not? Didn't you love each other?"

"Oh, yes. But you learn quickly that it takes a lot more than love to make a marriage!" Paula tossed a knowing glance in Liz's direction.

"You bet it does," Liz picked up, "which is the reason why we're all here! I've been thinking, though, that we haven't heard from our youngest couple yet. Dave and Kathy, you've been kind of quiet."

"We've been too busy listening to all you old folks!" laughed Dave.

"It's interesting hearing all the different issues," said Kathy, "and a little scary too. I never dreamed that there was so much to think about. I hope the rest of the weekend will be this informative."

Dave continued, "Since you asked what we talked about as we did the questionnaire, though, and since everyone seems to be real open here, I sometimes wonder whether the Church has anything new to say about premarital sex."

"Oh, Dave, you promised you wouldn't!" Kathy whispered and nudged him with her elbow.

"Why not?" said Dave, proceeding anyway. "It seems that so much else is changing in the Church these days."

"But not that, I'm afraid," returned Liz. "Take it from one happily married couple that there's a lot of wisdom in the traditional teaching. You may not be able to see it all now, but after you've been married a few years, you'll appreciate what I mean."

"What kind of wisdom?" Dave insisted.

"Well, apart from the obvious dangers of pregnancy and disease, and the possibility that one or both people might be using each other, there are some things that are not so obvious. Al and I talked about everything under the sun until we were married. Then sex seemed to take up all our communication time. It was almost like we had to learn all over again to talk things out with each other. The last thing you want to do is substitute sex for heart-to-heart verbal communication, especially before you're married. You've got too much to lose in terms of really getting to know each other."

"Hmm. I never looked at it that way," admitted Dave.

"And if I could give you a bit of motherly advice," said Liz, "keeping your young Romeo here at arm's length will make him more romantic, not less. Modern psychology is only just discovering that, but many women have known it for centuries!"

Everyone enjoyed the humor, but Janet gulped behind her smile. *Could that be the reason?* she wondered.

＊　＊　＊

"Thanks for seeing me right away, Father Benson," said Janet as she walked into the empty receptionist's office at the retreat center Saturday afternoon.

"Sure, Janet. Come on in and have a seat here while I go in and finish this phone call." He disappeared behind the door to his own office.

She tried to distract herself with a magazine, but the thoughts of the past few hours insisted on invading her solitude. Should she think them or should she put them out of her mind? After all, they were the reason she was here.

"Come on in," said Father Benson, opening the door to his office. The priest's sudden reappearance startled her, but Janet tried not to show it. "What's on your mind?" he said.

"I'm not quite sure where to begin," she said. "What's an annulment?"

"Wait a minute!" laughed Father Benson as he sat down in the armchair next to Janet. "You're not even married yet! Why this sudden interest in annulments?"

"The subject came up at our meeting this morning but only briefly. I was curious."

"Only curious?" The pastor sensed that his joviality might have been misplaced. "When you asked if we could talk right away there seemed to be something more on your mind."

"There is. Only I'm not sure what it is. It's all confusing. But I thought that if you could explain annulments to me that might help, since that's how this all began. Paula said that an annulment means you made a mistake about getting married. I always thought it was like a divorce for Catholics."

"Well, it's not really a Catholic divorce, that's for sure." Father Benson didn't realize that he had missed the clue Janet had given him. "You can't even file for an annulment until you're legally divorced. It's more like a determination, after the fact, that a failed marriage was invalid to begin with."

"That's what I meant. It was a mistake."

"Yes," the priest said slowly, "but it's a special kind of mistake. Most people make mistakes when they get married — they over-estimate or underestimate how much money their spouse is going to make, about how beautiful their wife is going to stay, about the best way to raise children — all sorts of mistakes. A marriage can't be annulled for just any reason."

"What kind of reason, then?" asked Janet.

"When I first studied canon law, the main reason was what they called 'the inability to fulfill the marriage contract.' Many of these reasons amounted to intentional deception, for example not reveal-ing that you were already married, not really being willing to have children, not intending to remain faithful to your spouse, and the like. In cases like that the injured party, so to speak, was entitled by Church law to have the contract declared null and void. Hence the name, annulment."

"That doesn't sound like what Paula was talking about," Janet countered.

"It wouldn't be right for me to reveal any more than she told you," said the pastor. "What did she say?"

"She made it sound like she got divorced because of poor communication between her and her first husband."

"Let me assure you that there was a lot more to it than that. Bad communication was part of it, but that's because good communica-tion is so essential to a marriage."

"I know that Hank, her first husband, drank a lot. She mentioned that later on in our discussion."

"Yes, he seems to have had that problem from the beginning too."

"You mean that alcoholism can annul a marriage?"

"That wouldn't be the right way to put it. Remember I said earlier that many of the traditional grounds for annulment amounted to intentional deception. That was before we knew anything about modern psychology. Today the Church recognizes that sometimes marriages are invalid due to unintentional deception."

"How can that be?"

"Sometimes people don't know it, but they're just fooling themselves. They believe they have what it takes to make a Christian marriage, but they really don't. The annulment process is a sad way to find out, after the fact, that a Christian marriage was doomed to failure from the start."

"You keep calling it a Christian marriage."

"It's the same as what we called a sacramental marriage at the group's first meeting last night. It's a marriage that's really happy and lasting — one that can be a sign to others of what God's love is like, as Liz put it; one that's based on caring and giving, on loving and serving each other."

Janet did not say anything for a few moments.

Father Benson asked softly, "Janet, are you wondering whether you or Bob might be making a mistake?"

The young woman tugged out a Kleenex from the box on the coffee table.

"You have time," Father Benson reassured her. "You both have lots of time — five months, at least. There's lots of time to talk it over."

If only Bob would take the time to talk! Janet thought to herself.

❄ ❄ ❄

Bob looked over the menu at Rigazzi's restaurant while Janet pondered on wedding plans. During the months after the weekend everything went well, as far as anyone on the outside could see. Janet added the flurry of wedding preparations to her already busy work schedule. The office had become short-handed just two months before the wedding. She still needed to find someone to redesign the sleeves and neckline of her gown. The bridesmaids' dresses *still* hadn't come in. Bob couldn't find time to help her address the invitations. She still had to make sure the wedding party would have places to stay. Bob left a lot of it to her, as he said he would. It was not so much that Janet minded, it was just that she would like to get some input from him from time to time.

Janet stared into the glass of Chablis in front of her. *But Bob is busier than I am,* she rationalized to herself. *When you're in retail marketing you start gearing up for Christmas in the fall.*

"Your apartment or mine?" The words sounded far away.

"Huh?" Janet realized she had been staring at the glass of wine in front of her. Lost in thought, she didn't even hear the noise of the restaurant.

"You've told me about all the wedding preparations," said Bob, "but one thing we haven't talked about is where we're going to live. Your apartment or mine?"

"I thought we had decided that a long time ago," said Janet, somewhat confused. "I've been dropping hints for wedding presents that would look nice in your place. A lot of my things I've already promised to my sister for when she moves out of my parents' house."

"That's right. I had forgotten that. It's just that in the past few months my place has gotten noisier. More people moving into the building with kids. They leave the halls messy too," Bob complained.

"I've noticed that, but I don't mind it."

"Well, I do," said Bob, "and I told the owner this morning that I may be moving out at the end of the month."

"Oh, Bob, you didn't!"

"Oh, yes, I did! Nothing definite, though, which is why I asked the question."

"But where would we *live*? And where would *you* live until we got married?"

"How about your place? Lots of couples do it these days, and with the money we'd save we could buy more furniture for a larger apartment in a nicer area."

"Oh, Bob, I don't want to do that. It would be like we're already married when we really aren't. Then the time after the wedding and the honeymoon would be a big letdown. Anyway, how would we explain it to Father Benson? He's going to be presiding at our wedding!"

"He doesn't have to know," Bob said blandly. "It's not as though you live in the same neighborhood as him."

"But it would be like…like lying," Janet protested. "Pretending to go along with what he's saying but doing the opposite!"

"Now, wait a minute, Janet. Who's the Catholic around here, anyway? I get along well with people, but that doesn't mean that I agree with everything they say. You know I went on that weekend just for your sake."

"I know, Bob, but you're not being fair! Just when I think I've got all the details straightened out, you spring this on me!"

"I'm sorry. It was just a thought. I was just thinking how nice it would be for me."

"For you?"

"For the both of us, I mean. It's not getting any warmer, you know. And one of us always has to drive home at night."

He's right, Janet thought. *It's not getting any warmer.*

❄ ❄ ❄

"You know, that weekend wasn't half as bad as I expected," Bob said to Al. Al and Liz had invited the couples from the weekend over to their house for a more informal, social get-together.

"Yeah, we really covered a lot of territory on those weekends," said Al. "When the groups are bigger it's exhausting, but with the small group we had when you were there it's a bit easier."

"For me, it was really interesting," said Dave, "and informative. I never realized there was so much to learn about expectations in marriage, money management, and getting along with in-laws. Not to mention sexuality. I think I'm finally beginning to figure women out!" He winked at his fiancée.

"When you do that," quipped Al, "write a book. It'll make you rich!"

"I sure like the way that you and Liz led the meetings in the program." Ray stood up and flexed his knee. "Lectures can always put me to sleep, but I can sit and talk all night if my leg doesn't stiffen up."

"What I liked was getting out of the house," said Paula, picking up her cup and saucer. "I've become such a homebody the past few years, and even when Ray comes over he usually helps the kids with their homework or watches TV with me. We're getting to be old married folks even before the wedding!"

"That's a good sign," said Al, helping her with the dishes.

"You don't have to convince *me,*" Paula said. "When I was married before, I lived in a constant state of tension."

Paula, Al, Liz, and Janet walked into the kitchen.

"Did I hear someone say 'tension'?" Janet asked as she set some dishes on the counter. "It seems to never let up! Pretty soon we'll be into Thanksgiving and the holidays, and I'm always finding more things that have to be done before the wedding."

"I suppose it's always harder the first time though," commented Paula, half-jokingly. "But it's also more exciting. Wouldn't you say so, Janet?"

"Too exciting, if you ask me," said Janet wearily. "Sometimes I don't know whether I'm coming or going."

"Now, wait a minute. That's my line," laughed Paula. "I'm the one with the four kids!"

"Bob seems to be taking it pretty well," Al noted, looking out at Ray and Bob in the living room.

"I don't think it means as much to a man as to a woman," Janet suggested.

"You mean you're having second thoughts?" Al queried as he began loading the dishwasher.

"I didn't say that," protested Janet.

"I'd say you were having second thoughts since the first day I saw you," said Al.

"Really, Al, that's a bit much to lay on Janet now," interjected Liz. "We all have second thoughts."

Al closed the dishwasher door and turned on the machine. "I'm going to check and see if we left any other dishes in the living room," Al said as he left the room.

Paula said, "Maybe it's time for a little heart-to-heart talk here, where the men in the other room can't hear us."

Kathy, Liz, Paula, and Janet sat down at the kitchen table.

"I don't quite know how to say this but…. Well I'll just come out with it," said Liz. "Janet, are you pregnant?"

"Oh, no, it's not that!" Janet was taken aback by her bluntness.

"What is it, then?" said Liz. "Marriage is too beautiful a thing for someone to be behaving the way you do. I've seen dozens of couples go through this program, and by now my woman's intuition has been confirmed more than once. Most people get happier, albeit more frazzled, as the wedding day approaches. Some don't, though."

"And I'm one of them, I guess," said Janet weakly.

Paula put her arm on Janet's shoulder. Janet held back tears.

"Have you talked with Bob about this?" asked Liz gently.

"If I could, I don't think I'd feel this way."

❋ ❋ ❋

"What do you mean, 'no more'?" Bob said, trying to adjust to Janet's announcement while still keeping his mind on driving. "It's been OK with you ever since we were engaged! Here we are now, two months from the wedding, and suddenly it's not all right. What's gotten into you?"

Janet searched for the right words. "It's not so much what's gotten into me. It's been in me for a long time. I just felt I had to get it out."

"But why now?" Bob shot back.

"Because it's now…or never."

Bob put on the brakes and pulled over to the curb. "What do you mean, *never*? You mean you'd call off the wedding after all this?"

"I'm not sure what I mean, exactly," said Janet. "It's just that I feel I need the space."

"I'm not getting your drift. The space for what?"

"The space to get to know you better — the space to get to know the man I'm going to marry."

"Janet, you know me better than anybody else. Certainly better than anyone I've ever dated."

"Sometimes I don't feel that way at all, Bob."

"What makes you say that?"

"Remember on that weekend when we had that questionnaire to do?"

"The paperwork. Sure, I remember. What about it?"

"You told me things then that you had never said before, and we haven't had a talk like that together since. I felt so close to you then, closer than when we first fell in love. Didn't you feel it too?"

"Yeah, I felt it. But…"

"But what?" said Janet, looking at him with wide eyes.

"I thought it was just a passing thing."

"I haven't felt that way with you since. And I want to, Bob, I really want to."

"And so?"

"And so, I'm asking if you would work on that with me. Use our time to get to know each other better. Get closer to each other."

"Hey, c'mon, if we haven't been close, I don't know what 'close' means!"

"I'm *serious*, Bob. Sex isn't the kind of closeness that I'm talking about. I want us to go and talk with a counselor that Father Benson recommended."

"Hey, c'mon, I don't have time for that. We're in the heat of gearing up for Christmas at work. I just don't have the time. Anyway, I have to work these extra long days right now. No counselor would be able to meet us with our crazy hours."

"Well then, I think we'd better postpone the wedding until we *have* the time."

"Postpone the wedding! Are you crazy?" Bob hollered.

"Actually, for the first time since August I'm feeling sane," said Janet. "I think I know now what I want from marriage. I think I know now what I need from the man I love."

"So if we go to the counselor you'll still go through with the wedding?" asked Bob.

"I'm not making any promises."

"What's that supposed to mean?"

"It means I want to be *sure*, Bob. I want to be as sure as I can be that we can make it through a whole lifetime together. I may know that after we visit the counselor a few times, but I may not. I don't want us to make a mistake."

"Honey, we're not making a mistake. Believe me. I'll take good care of you," Bob said as he placed his hand on her shoulder.

"I need to know that for myself, Bob. I need to be as sure as I can be. I just need the space."

Bob looked into her eyes and saw tears. "Sure, babe, anything you need. But tell me one thing. Is there room in that space for a kiss?"

"Uh-huh," she said, moving closer to him. He kissed her, and she reached up to hug him as tightly as she could. Tears trickled down her cheeks. She looked out the rear windshield at the suburban street winding out behind them. She squeezed her eyes shut to help hold back the tears and thought about how far they had come...and how far they still had to go.

What Are We Getting Into?

The people in the O'Reillys' kitchen had just finished lunch, and they were supposed to be making the final plans for the big family gathering tomorrow after the ordinations. As usual, their conversation wandered in other directions, but that's the way it was with the O'Reillys.

"Well, tomorrow's the big day," said Larry O'Reilly as he cleared away lunch dishes from the table. His brother, T.J., sat at the table and smoked a cigarette for dessert.

"I'm glad it worked out this way, Uncle Larry," said Tom, T.J.'s son.

"What do you mean?"

"Being ordained on the same day as you. You think the family can handle both a priest *and* a permanent deacon?"

"Tom, I'm sure having two ordained men in the family isn't going to kill us off!"

Irene said, "I suppose that it *is* sort of nice. It couldn't have happened thirty years ago when I was your age. In those days the diaconate was just another step on the road to the priesthood. I'm sure glad Larry didn't decide to become a deacon *then*," said Irene. "If he did, I could never have married him."

"I'm glad too, dear," said Larry, "although I *did* think about becoming a priest once or twice. Old Father Shaughnessy was always trying to lure me into the seminary. The priesthood was always Father Shaughnessy's idea, not God's or mine. It just wouldn't have been right for me. At least Tom can't say I ever tempted *him* to be a priest! No family, lonely old rectory…. Nope, that just wasn't for me. It's not an easy life you're choosing, son."

"Oh, Larry," said Irene. "Must you always be so paternalistic? Just because Tom won't carry on the O'Reilly name, you've got no right to complain. Your two daughters have already given you three beautiful grandchildren."

"Sorry," interjected Tom. "We can't all do everything. Someday the Church may change the celibacy rules sort of like it happened after Vatican II with allowing permanent deacons to be married. But I'm sure this is what God is calling me to, and the life of a priest has its own rewards."

Tom's father, T.J., took a long drag on his cigarette and said, "The thing I still can't figure out is why it takes so long to become a priest. It takes more time than it takes to go to law school!"

"Well, it *is* a lifetime commitment, Pop. The Church wants young men to experience celibacy for a while before making their final promises. I'll only be twenty-five when I'm ordained, but in some religious orders like the Jesuits some men don't make their final vows until they're in their thirties. Besides, the year of internship gives us a good idea of what parish life is like so that we can be sure this is what we really want."

"I still don't see it. The Church allows people to get married a lot sooner than that, and that's a lifetime commitment too!"

"Sure, but look at the divorce rate," said Uncle Larry, "Maybe if the Church made young people wait longer and prepare better for marriage, more marriages would last."

"What about it, T.J.?" Larry asked his brother, Tom's father, "Do you think you would have waited five years for Mary?"

"Hell, no! We'd have eloped! But that's just my point. A lot of priests leave the ministry anyway, don't they?"

"In the sixties and seventies the dropout rate got pretty high — twenty percent according to some estimates — but it's way below that now. Today it's nowhere near the estimated divorce rate. Most men who leave today leave during their seminary years — before they're even priests. From that point of view, it's a pretty good system."

"Fine," said T.J., "but what about all that schooling? What did you need that for? It's not as though you were becoming a brain surgeon or something."

"Oh, T.J.," said Mary, "just because you went into business right after high school doesn't mean that education isn't helpful. Lots of professional people these days go to school for two to five years after college to get the degrees they need. Years and years of education isn't just for doctors and lawyers."

"As a matter of fact," said Larry, "I wish I had been able to get at least a year's leave with pay while studying for the diaconate. Going to school two nights a week for four years is pretty rugged for a man my age. Even the 'boys' in our diaconate classes — the ones who were the minimum age of thirty-five — felt it was a pretty rigorous training schedule."

"What could you possibly have studied all those years?" T.J. asked his brother. "Maybe youngsters like Tom here need to learn some things before the bishop turns them loose in a parish, but you're already a successful executive."

"To some extent you're right," admitted Larry. "Deacon candidates get about two years of graduate education spread out over four years, since we go to school only part-time. But not all the men in the diaconate program are into management; which, incidentally, is a skill that most of us will need in parish work. The principal training that we got was theological and pastoral — a lot like Tom's. It covers things I never heard of when I was getting my bachelor's degree in business administration."

Mary's eyes lit up. "Oh, I remember. Tom once showed us a description of his seminary program. It had courses like 'Old Testament Themes' and 'Theology of the Sacraments.' He learned about Church history and canon law...."

"Not to mention Christology and ecclesiology and morality," added Tom. "And don't forget those other courses like psychology, sociology, and economics or the practical courses like administration, counseling, and homiletics. Most priests and deacons have to run some parish programs, and they often help people with their problems. We all have to preach. You'd want us to be prepared to give good sermons, wouldn't you, Pop?"

"Judging from some of the sermons I've heard in my life," said T.J., "I'd guess that not everybody passes that course!"

"Oh, for goodness sake, T.J.! They're only men, just like you," his wife insisted. "The first two businesses you started lost more money than they made. Give these men a chance to learn, just like you had to."

Her son took up her argument, "That's one of my pet peeves about the ministry. People seem to expect us to be perfect, to be always batting a thousand. But when priests and deacons are ordained, they don't stop being *men*. We've got just as many faults and failings as the next guy."

"You don't have to tell *me*," said Larry, rinsing dishes and handing them to his wife to dry. "Sometimes when I was studying for all those courses I wished I was a lot smarter."

"Fortunately, he didn't have to do it alone. He had me to help him," said Irene.

"How could you have helped him?" asked T.J.

Irene replied, "Many of the courses that Larry took were open to both deacon candidates and their wives. I talked with Mary about it lots of times. She liked hearing about it, because it helped her understand what Tom was learning in his training for the priesthood."

"You mean you got almost all the same training that Larry did, and yet tomorrow he'll be ordained and you won't?" said T.J., seeming alarmed.

"Since when did *you* become a feminist?" chided Mary.

"I never said I was in favor of women becoming priests," answered T.J. "But deaconesses I could take, I think. After all, what would be the difference between a deaconess and a nun, except that nuns aren't married?"

"The main difference, as I understand it," offered Irene, "is that nuns, or Sisters, are not ordained. They take vows like monks and Brothers in religious orders do, but that doesn't make them priests. After all, becoming a deacon is almost like being a priest, except that a deacon can't do everything that a priest can do. Nuns are not allowed to preach at Mass or administer the sacraments, which are the main functions of the deacon in the Church."

"Oh, I see," said T.J. "You mean that if the Church allowed women to be deacons, then it might have to allow them to be priests as well. And who knows, pretty soon it might have to deal with women wanting to be bishops! In that case, I guess the Church is right, not allowing women to be deacons. Give 'em an inch and they'll take a yard!"

"T.J.!" Mary said and sighed. "Personally, I think you were right the first time. Irene tells me that some of the deacons' wives see the inequity of the situation and don't see why they couldn't be ordained. Tom, weren't there women deacons in the early Church?"

"Well, sure, in the first few hundred years. Theoretically, the Church could reinstate the order of deaconesses just as it has restored the diaconate as an office in the Church," said Tom. "But right now the Church sort of works like a family in the sense that in a family everybody can't do everything. Usually each person in a family is better at one thing than the others are, and so that person does that one thing. In a family everybody has a certain role, and as long as everyone respects everyone else's role, things run smoothly. In theory, there's no reason why men and women couldn't reverse the traditional roles of breadwinner and homemaker, so that the women would go out to work while the men stayed home and raised the children."

"That's already changing in many families," his mother pointed out.

"Right," said Tom. But my point is that in any family, everybody can't do everything. There has to be a certain division of labor. And it's the same in the Church. Theoretically, any priest can confirm or even ordain."

"So what you are saying, Tom," said Mary, "is that although your father and I have accepted the traditional husband-wife roles in our family, it doesn't have to be that way. In your sisters' families, for example, they and their husbands might arrange things a little differently."

"Right," continued Tom. "And so in the future the Church could conceivably allow married deacons to function as priests or even as bishops, and that's the reason that many people are against women's ordination as deacons. It would admit the possibility that somewhere along the road women could also be allowed to function as priests, which is currently not allowed in the Church and which the present pope does not believe is allowable."

"Do you think it will ever be allowed?" asked Irene.

"I think that's something for history and the Holy Spirit to decide," replied Tom. "If it's God's wish, it will happen.

"A similar argument could be made about allowing priests to marry. Most priests were married in the early centuries of the Church, and it was not until the Middle Ages that celibacy became the rule for priests. But I'm not living in the early Church; I'm living in a time when deciding to serve God and his people as a priest means I have to agree to the rule of celibacy. It's like when I was a teenager I realized I had two choices. I could run away from home and do whatever I wanted, or I could stay with my family and live according to the rules laid down for us."

"You got it exactly right," said T.J. "Why, I can remember when you were fifteen and started to get uppity…."

"I don't think we have to go over all that again, Pop. Getting back to what I was saying," said Tom, "I realized at one point that if I wanted to be a contributing member of this family, I had to abide by the rules of the house. And it's the same with the priesthood or the diaconate or with people in religious orders or with laypeople in the Church. There's so much good that we can do within the way things are. Sure, we can push to change the rules within the Church, but that's a different issue. That's the issue of authority within the Church. But ordination is not about authority, it's about service."

"That's the way I look at it too," said Larry. "I've worked in a number of different companies, but in each one I've had to ask myself, 'Is this the job I really want to do?' At this point in my life, then, I want to be of special service to the Church, and I came to the realization that the best way to use my gifts and talents in the service of the Church would be as a deacon. I guess you could name that a 'calling' or a 'vocation.' But it's just the way I feel called by God to serve the people in the Church right now."

"So how will ordination make you any different from the rest of us?" prodded T.J. He looked at his son and said, "You'll still be 'my son Tom' to me."

"I don't think ordination makes me any different as a human being. I'll still be the same old me with all my abilities and shortcomings. But it makes me different as a member of the Church. It gives me an ability to serve people in ways that I couldn't if I weren't a priest."

"When I was young my parents told me about 'priestly powers' as if they were something special and mysterious," said Mary.

"Well, they are special, but they're not mysterious. *Power* is just another word for ability. If we have the power to do something, we have the ability to do it. Right now, as a layperson, you have the ability to do many things in the Church."

"You mean like being a lector or a religion teacher?" asked T.J.

"Right. But the crucial thing is that this power is not power for its own sake. It's a special ability to serve the Church in specific ways."

"Well, where does all this power come from?" T.J. pressed him.

"Ultimately, of course, it comes from God. But it doesn't come from God directly. God doesn't go around zapping people and turning them into priests. It comes through the Church. That's why the bishop is the only one empowered in the Church to perform ordinations. The bishop is the representative of the Church in any particular locality. So the bishop acts on behalf of the people in his diocese when he ordains men to serve them as priests."

"Wait a minute," announced T.J. "I'm beginning to see something here. You said that the power to be a priest comes through the Church."

"That's right."

"But aren't *we* the Church? We the *people*, I mean."

"So?" said Tom, wondering where his father was leading.

"So the way I see it," said T.J., "if we're the Church, then we're giving you the power to be a priest for us. That means I'm still the boss. You'll be working for me!"

"Right. Priests are ordained to serve the people of God in the Church. In a sense, they're the boss. The priest serves the people in his parish, and the bishop serves the priests and people in his diocese. Even the pope calls himself *servus servorum Dei,* 'servant of the servants of God.' It's all a ministry of service."

❄ ❄ ❄

Tom stared at the ceiling from his bed back at his parents' house. Crickets chirped. The squealing tires of some kid hot-rodding over on Grand Avenue started Tom thinking about who he might have been had he not chosen to be a priest.

Did I make it sound too easy? he thought, recalling the little lecture he'd given his parents, aunt, and uncle the previous afternoon. *It's easy to explain the theory behind the priesthood, but it's another thing to live it.* And tomorrow he would take that step that would change his life forever.

Oh, Lord; I'm sure engaged couples feel the same way — wondering if they're taking the right step or making a mistake about getting married, he argued with himself. But the thought was not reassuring. The fact that other people made hard decisions every day didn't make his own any easier. And anyhow, lots of people made the wrong decision about whom to marry or else the diocesan marriage tribunal wouldn't have so many annulment case files piling up on the desks.

People always expect priests to have it all together. No doubts about vocation allowed. No doubts about faith allowed. But he sometimes *had* those doubts. He'd been perfectly sure of his calling when he entered the seminary after college. He'd been thinking about the priesthood for years, and slowly he had grown more certain that this was what God wanted him to do with his life.

How did it start? Where did it begin, this feeling that I ought to be a priest? Certainly his family had a lot to do with it. His mother had made religion a part of the family's life. She used to pray with him, after reading from *Grimm's Fairy Tales* or *Pinnochio.* They'd always said grace before meals to remind them all of God's providence. Mom had hung a crucifix above his bed and sometimes brought Christian art and posters home from the Catholic Supply store. Tom remembered all the typical things of Catholic childhood — the manger scene beneath the Christmas tree, meatless meals in Lent. Mom had so many subtle yet constant reminders of how important God was for her and how important she wanted religion to be for her children.

And Pop...although he had as much tact and grace as a baby elephant, he too had been a good example of what it meant to live a Christian life. T.J. didn't question the Church's teachings much because he seemed to instinctively know they were on the right track. "Practice what you preach," Pop always said, "because if it ain't worth trying it ain't worth believing." Pop...the man of action, coaching the kids' softball team and helping with the scout troop when they went camping. He was the perennial usher at ten o'clock Mass and chief cook at the annual First Communion breakfast. He had shown Tom and his sisters that helping others could be fun. Indeed, Pop had always seemed happiest when he was doing something for someone else.

Tom turned over in the bed and remembered Monsignor Bandinelli, who had been anything but an inspiration. He had seemed so different. Distant. He wore his cassock like China wore the Great Wall — to keep out petty intruders like little Tommy O'Reilly. Monsignor Bandinelli used to scare Tom; the old man never smiled. Yet as Tom got older the monsignor's mysterious cloak of priesthood came to have an attractiveness of its own. But it was the younger priests like Father Dave, fresh out of the seminary and filled with new ideas, who had first made ordained life look so romantic. Father Dave was always there when you needed him —

always with a smile, a good word, a listening ear. Tom had wanted to follow in Father Dave's footsteps. The young seminarian nearly worshiped the fresh young priest to whom everyone flocked. But Tom's idolatry tumbled and shattered when four years ago Dave left the priesthood and got married.

"A crisis of vocation," Tom's spiritual director had called it.

Crisis, hell! Tom thought. *It almost drove me crazy! Why didn't Dave at least try to explain it to us?* The event made Tom doubt not just his vocation but himself, the Church, even God.

In bed that night, Tom slowly assembled his life, as though it were a jigsaw puzzle with interlocking pieces. He remembered he wanted to be a priest so he could help people feel better about themselves when they had sinned; so he could help explain to people what Christ's words meant; so Pop could be proud of "the baby of the family." Tom began to realize that the Church, like any other institution, had built-in frustrations that sooner or later he, too, would have to face. He began to come to terms with a God who did not always see things his way, and who did not always make things work out the way we wanted them to be.

Did his mother or his father ever have such doubts? If they did, they didn't talk about it. That's partly what had made it so hard for him the first time, not having a model (if you could call it that) of doubt as well as one of faith. But by sharing his soul-searching with others, he discovered he was not alone. Many of the men that he was studying with had gone through similar experiences, for their own reasons. Faith, he learned, sometimes had to grope in darkness. But it helped to have someone share that scary journey with him — someone who had been there before.

Tom tossed and turned some more in the bed. He thought about celibacy. It wasn't living without sex that bothered him as much as living without someone to share life with. Oh sure, he had his fun with girls in college, but even after he'd gotten over feeling guilty about it, he decided that wasn't really what he was looking for. He was looking for something deeper, something more permanent.

But could he handle living alone? For all his brave talk defending the Church's practice, Tom realized that celibacy had originally not meant living alone. It had been a practice of men living together in monasteries, not living separately in rectories. Today, though, the community dimension of the celibate life had been forgotten, leaving priests to make it through life on their own. Now, with the shortage of priests worsening, the prospect of being the only priest in a parish meant he might not have even male companionship around the dinner table. And he hated watching TV alone.

So celibacy did worry him, though not for the reason most people thought. Many of the older priests he had gotten to know did not seem to be really happy men. Some even turned to the bottle every night to drown their loneliness. Some, like Dave, gave up trying and decided to get married.

Yet marriage was not an easy answer either. Tom knew that married people are often just as lonely as celibates, maybe even more often, judging by the divorce rate. He knew they get frustrated, too, when they realize that the bud of romance is not blossoming into any kind of deeper union with their spouse. *Stuck with a stranger for life. It happens. Thank God Mom and Dad aren't like that.* They were two very different people, but somehow they had learned to talk and reveal their feelings to each other. It was from them that he had learned the value of companionship and communication.

One of the benefits of ministry, he had come to learn in his year in the diaconate, was that there were always people around who were willing to talk. Even on vacation, once they learned that you were a priest, they'd tell you their life story. The hard part was finding people who were willing to listen to *your* story when you needed to unburden yourself. But it could be done. Priests who were well adjusted always seemed to have a few special friends with whom they could kick off their shoes if they had to. But the happiest priests, Tom thought, were the ones who had found a way to develop an extended family relationship with the people in their parish. If he couldn't be a husband, he could always be a brother to people who would invite him to their homes. If he couldn't be a father, he could always be an uncle to their kids. There were many ways to avoid the potential isolation of the rectory. But you had to work at it. If you did not let people know you needed them, they assumed that you were pretty self-sufficient living alone. *But you're not*, Tom reminded himself.

Another thing he'd noticed about the priests who seemed to be the happiest in their ministry was that they shared their work with others. They didn't try to meet all the spiritual needs in their parish, but instead they worked at enabling others to meet those needs — multiplying their own effectiveness many times over. And by developing a team ministry they created an important support group with whom they could pray and talk — people with whom they could share their hopes, doubts, joys, and frustrations in trying to serve God's people. That's something else he needed to work at, Tom decided. A parish staff does not become a community just because they all get paid out of the same collection basket.

And yet none of these relationships, rewarding as they might be, was permanent. He had entered the seminary five years before, so sure that he had found God and that God was calling him to the priesthood. What could be more permanent than God? Isn't God supposed to be eternal and unchanging? Or what could be more stable than the priesthood? Isn't the priesthood something that is received once and for all, like Baptism?

Within those few years in the seminary, though, Tom's idealistic vision of priestly life had crumbled. Examining the wreckage, he discovered pieces of the God he used to believe in. The old God lay there in ruins. Totally. But for some reason, he did not pack up and leave the seminary then and there. Something, or someone, told him to wait. It held him in the middle of the storm. And when the wind died down, it led him by the hand through the desert night.

Before that had happened, Tom recalled, he thought he knew how to pray. But at that point in his life prayer seemed like just a bunch of words spoken to a statue. He'd made so many promises, so many petitions; and he'd offered them without waiting for an answer. Finally he did not know any longer who or what he was addressing — if there was really anything out there. He did not know any longer what to say or if there was any purpose to it.

Finally, he decided to listen.

What came to him in the silence was not an answer, but a promise. Not a vision, but an invitation — an invitation to keep walking on a journey begun many years before. Tom knew he had to keep going, even though he no longer knew exactly *where* he was going. The invitation urged him to keep walking through the night, for every night is followed by daylight and every day followed by night in the ongoing cycle that was, and is, life.

Tom just wasn't so sure now, as he once had been, of the road that stretched out before him. He was not sure that the priesthood was the only way to go. He was not sure whether he could stand the clerical bureaucracy of the Church or the loneliness or living up to the expectations of people whom he feared would believe he was

Superpriest — able to leap dark nights of the soul in a single bound. *I'm going to wear a collar, not a cape!* he thought.

But he was sure he had done the right thing by staying in the seminary. And he was pretty sure that he was following the way that God was leading him right now. Tomorrow was another day. Tomorrow was the day he would take the next step in his journey of listening to the One who was calling.

❄ ❄ ❄

Larry finished his second cup of coffee over a glazed doughnut. Irene hid behind the morning paper reading the weather forecast. "There's only a twenty percent chance of rain," she said.

"Uh-huh," said Larry as he stared blankly into his empty cup. "You know," he finally said, "I couldn't fall asleep last night."

Irene lowered the newspaper and said, "I could tell that you were restless. What was bothering you?"

"Nothing really. No, I shouldn't say that. I was thinking, and since I couldn't stop it, I guess you could say I was bothered by it."

"Thinking about the ceremony today, right?"

"Yeah. I wonder a little about what I'm getting myself, and you, into."

"Haven't we been through all that before?"

"Sure. But it still bugs me. And I know it worries some of the other guys in the diaconate class. On the other hand, there are the guys who couldn't care less. They just want to get the bishop's hands laid on them so that they can get out there in the parish and do their thing. I wish I could be as gung-ho about it as they are."

"If you were, you wouldn't be yourself, and I wouldn't have married you. I admired your pensiveness and the way you looked at things from every angle, always giving all sides a fair shake."

Larry smiled. "Thanks, I needed that. Especially today. But I always knew that a beauty like you wouldn't fall in love with me for my looks." He looked at her. "You're getting better with age, darling, like vintage wine."

"Why *thank* you!" she said. "But I've enjoyed becoming more intellectual too, like the man I love."

"And you are, you know," said Larry. "You asked better questions than any of the other women in the classes, and I noticed that the teachers always took your ideas seriously."

"Thanks for the compliment. Now, what were you thinking about last night?"

"I still don't like it," said Larry. "This whole deacon thing is still too indefinite, still too in-between."

"You mean that a deacon is neither a priest nor a layman, but vaguely somehow both?"

"Yes, but it's more than that. It has to do with Holy Orders, which I suppose is why I was thinking about it again last night. What does ordination give us that we wouldn't have if we were not ordained?"

"Isn't it supposed to give you some sort of special grace?" Irene suggested, remembering what she had learned in one of the theology courses.

"Even if it does, I'm sure that God would give all the help deacons need to perform their ministry, whether or not they've been through a special ceremony. I don't see God withholding grace just because someone hasn't said the right words!"

"You're getting cynical again, dear. You promised you'd try not to be."

"Sorry, I was thinking of the situation that Al Cranston got himself into when he was ordained a deacon a few years back. His first pastor was a fine man, but the one they sent to the parish after him kept reminding Al that 'only priests have the power to do this,' and 'deacons don't have the power to do that.' "

"So it's a matter of power, then?" asked Irene. "Divine power versus ecclesiastical power."

"Both, I guess. But some people don't realize that all that 'power' language has been taken out of the old ordination rite and replaced in the new ceremony with words that speak mainly of service and commitment. And that's not only for ordination to the diaconate, it's for priestly ordination too."

"All right, let's say, then, that ordination does not give you any special or supernatural powers. So what?"

"That's exactly my point. What does ordination give us that we don't already have?"

"I remember when we rehearsed the ordination ceremony that the text said something about 'being raised to the order of deacons,' " Irene said.

"That's like becoming a lieutenant or a captain without getting any special commission," Larry countered.

"Well, what's wrong with that? The Church is organized much

like the army. The pope is the commander-in-chief, bishops are sort of like generals, priests are maybe colonels or majors...."

"That puts deacons at the bottom of the pecking order...."

"I disagree," said Irene. "We haven't gotten to the *lay*people, yet."

"You mean like the parish organist or the parish council officers or the catechists?" asked Larry.

"Well, yes, but there's even more. At the bottom are all the privates who're just putting in their time, sitting in the pews."

"I don't really like that image of the Church," said Larry. "Why do *any* of us have to be 'better' than the others?"

"I don't like the structure either," admitted Irene, "but it fits the present authority structure in the Church, which evolved at a time when the main model of authority was the Roman Empire, with its various orders of government officials."

"Hey, that's right!" Larry said, remembering when they covered the topic in a Church history class. "I forgot all about that. OK, so the 'Holy Orders' in the Church developed in a parallel way to the 'secular orders' of the civil government. What of it?"

"Well, in the army couldn't you be a captain without having any special job to do? I mean, couldn't you have a rank without having a specific commission?"

"Sure, you just move from one assignment to another, but you never lose your rank, and your assignments are always proper to your rank."

"So why couldn't service in the Church be like that too? You could look at being a deacon like moving from being a noncom to a commissioned officer, without a specific assignment."

"You sound like you've got the lingo down pat!"

"Hey, I was an army brat, remember?" Irene joked. "My daddy made it up through the ranks the hard way, and our family heard all about it every step of the way!"

"What you're saying, then, is that being ordained a deacon is like being given a certain rank, with the clergy being something like the commissioned officers in the Church. But having that rank doesn't give you any specific assignment."

"That's right. And that would explain why deacons do so many different things in the Church. Some do parish administration, some do catechetical work, some do pastoral ministry in hospitals and other places. You name it, and deacons are into it."

"That's fine, except for one thing. Every deacon can serve at the altar with the priest, preach, and administer certain sacraments. So some specific duties *do* seem to come with ordination."

"Every analogy has its shortcomings," said Irene. "But why not think of them as privileges, rather than duties? Sort of like eating at the officers' table or being eligible for some assignments that noncoms aren't allowed to take, even if they've got the talents for them, just because they don't have the rank."

"You know, I think you're right. Looking at the duties of the diaconate as privileges fits in a whole lot better with this idea that deacons are ordained to serve, not to have power over people."

"Sure. It means that more can be asked of you once you're ordained than could be asked of someone who is not ordained. But in the Lord's way of looking at things, service is a privilege, not a duty. Didn't Jesus say that whoever would be first among us must be a servant to all? To me, that means that the more service you give to others, the higher up you are in the kingdom, and that's a privilege."

"Irene, you're a theological genius! I can't wait until I tell the other deacon candidates about this! We've probably spent more hours arguing about where the diaconate fits in the Church than any other single problem. You might have the answer."

"Well, actually, I thought about it before," she said.

"You did? When?"

"When I heard you guys discussing it hour after hour. I just figured you had to be overlooking something. Woman's intuition."

"But what gave you the idea of turning the whole problem upside down and looking at the responsibilities of the diaconate not as duties but as privileges?"

"Well, to be truthful, the idea came to me in that canon law class when Father Schmitt was going over the section on 'the duties of the wife to the husband' in sexual matters."

"So?"

"So I looked at him and said to myself, 'Making love to my man ain't no *duty*, Father, it's a *privilege*!' "

❊　❊　❊

T.J. insisted that they get to the cathedral early so they could get seats with a good view. Even with a large number of visitors attending, however, the church was so spacious that it was not filled to capacity. It would have been surprising if it was on this Saturday morning. The grandchildren kept wiggling impatiently and asking, "When's it going to start?" Mary turned around and saw Irene getting into the pew behind her with the members of her family.

The organist began playing as the procession started. Everyone in the cathedral rose to greet the candidates. First came the seventeen deacon candidates in their white albs, followed by the four candidates for priesthood, already wearing the stole that was the sign of their diaconate. By the end of the morning, the new deacons would all wear stoles, and the new priests would wear chasubles.

"Wow! Look at all those priests!" said the youngest O'Reilly, Joseph.

"That's because this is a very special day," said his grandfather, T.J. "Do you see that man at the end? Do you know who he is?"

"The one with the big pointy hat? He must be really old. He's walking with a big cane," said Joseph.

"That's the bishop," said T.J., smiling. "He's the one who's going to ordain your Uncle Tom and my brother Larry."

When Bishop Morrison took his place at the presidential chair behind the altar, an attendant accepted his ceremonial miter and crosier.

"Welcome," he began, extending his arms in greeting, "to this most important day when we shall be ordaining twenty-one men to the service of the Church. Our diocesan chancellor, Monsignor Wetzel, will be delivering the sermon, so before we begin I would like to say how thankful I am to all of you who have made this day possible.

"Without the loving support of their families and friends, these men could not be here today. Without the dedicated teachers in the seminary, they would not be as well prepared as they are for their ministry in our diocese. And without all of you who contributed so generously to the Church, they would be less able to perform the work to which they have dedicated themselves.

"This happy day is a celebration not only for the candidates who stand before you, but it is a day of celebration for all of us. Let us begin our celebration, then, in the name of the Father, and of the Son, and of the Holy Spirit." At the conclusion of the Gospel reading, however, Bishop Morrison again donned his miter as he sat down in his chair.

"Those to be ordained, please rise and indicate your presence when your name is called," announced the master of ceremonies.

One by one, the candidates rose and said "Present" when they heard their names, after which the bishop was formally requested in the name of the Church to ordain them as deacons and priests. When he gave his permission, they all sat down again, and Monsignor Wetzel stepped up to the pulpit.

"This is an important day for all of us," said the monsignor, "especially for the three groups of candidates whom the bishop has just formally consented to ordain. Three young men who will be ordained to the diaconate today will go on next year to the priesthood, God willing. Fourteen men will today be ordained to the permanent diaconate and begin a new life of service in various parishes and diocesan agencies. Finally, four deacons who have just completed their year of internship will go on today to take the final step toward serving God as priests.

"In the years following the Second Vatican Council we have witnessed a great expansion in ministry to the life of God in the Church. Under the inspiration of the Holy Spirit, the Council approved the reinstitution of the office of the permanent diaconate at a time when no one could humanly foresee the great changes that would take place in the ensuing decades. Thirty years ago, fifteen men were ordained to the priesthood in this cathedral, at a time when priests were practically the only people dedicated to the service of the Church, apart from Sisters and Brothers in religious orders. Today, the Lord has given us twenty-one men who have responded to a calling to serve the Church. Naturally, we must not forget the many dedicated laypeople who today serve the Church in a great variety of positions. God has been very good to us in calling forth so many to enrich the life of the Church.

"Today, however, we celebrate a different kind of dedication to service in the Church, a dedication which is permanent. The candidates who have just been presented for ordination have expressed their willingness to devote their talents to the service of God's people, not just for a time but for always. They may serve in a variety of capacities in parishes and the diocese, but they want to be permanently available to the Church for as long as there are people who need them. For this reason they are elevated to the diaconate and the priesthood.

"The Greek word *diakonos* literally means "servant." Those who are raised to the order of diaconate, therefore, are commissioned permanently to the service of the Church. Unlike the many laypeople who serve in parishes, schools, and other Church institutions, however, deacons serve the Church at the discretion of the bishop. They serve under the principal pastor and teacher of the diocese, extending his own ministry in a special way to all the people in his care. For this reason the bishop gives them the authority to perform many functions that, in ancient times when the Church was much smaller, the bishop himself performed. He authorizes them to preach the Gospel at Mass and to lead other forms of public worship. He authorizes them to assist at the liturgy in a special capacity — to baptize people, to witness weddings, and to officiate at funerals.

"Priests, too, as is clear from today's celebration, are deacons who have been ordained to serve. But they also take a further step toward serving the Church on behalf of the bishop. They commit themselves to a life of celibacy in order to be more readily available to those who need them. A priest has been defined as a 'mediator between God and people,' and in this respect priests participate in the bishop's pastoral responsibility to make God available to people and to bring people closer to God. They offer the sacrifice of Christ's body and blood to God in the Eucharistic liturgy. They reconcile sinners to God and the Church in the sacrament of Reconciliation, and they extend divine healing to those who are ill in the Anointing of the Sick. Deacons and priests, therefore, are unique among the Church's ministers because they are ordained by the bishop to serve in his name, as extensions of his own pastoral and sacramental ministry to the People of God. But they are like all other ministers, lay and religious, in the Church, in that they need your constant prayers and support in order to succeed in what they have dedicated their lives to doing.

Monsignor Wetzel turned to the candidates. "And you, my brothers, who are about to be sealed by the laying on of hands to a life of dedicated service, must always be mindful of the two pillars on which your future ministry rests. On the one side it rests on the authority of the bishop, by whose consent and for whose work you will be ordained as deacons and priests in this diocese. On the other side it rests on the needs of the faithful, who ask and who indeed have a right to be served by men who are willing to put the needs of others ahead of their own personal desires.

"Both of those pillars, however, ultimately rest on only one foundation, which is Christ our Lord. It is Jesus who established the Church as a means of divine life for all places and times. It is Jesus who gives you both the model of ministry to live up to and the grace to live up to it in your daily lives. It is Jesus who lives in the Church, his Body, inspiring its leaders and guiding its people to work together for the salvation of the world. Pray, therefore, that you will be worthy to serve faithfully, so that when you meet the Lord face-to-face you will hear him say, 'Well done, my good and faithful servant....Come, share your master's joy.' "

After the homily everyone paused in silence for a few moments, reflecting on the message they had heard, before the master of ceremonies signaled the candidates to rise for their formal examination by the bishop.

Speaking first to the deacon candidates and then to the priest candidates, Bishop Morrison addressed a series of questions to them which were similar to the questions that candidates for Baptism and Confirmation answer. He first spoke to the unordained men: "Are you resolved to discharge the office of deacon with humility and love in order to assist the bishop and the priests and to serve the people of Christ?"

To this question and the others following it, the deacon candidates said "I do" in unison.

Turning next to the deacons who were about to be ordained priests the bishop asked: "Are you resolved, with the help of the Holy Spirit, to discharge without fail the office of priesthood in the presbyterial order as conscientious fellow workers with the bishops in caring for the Lord's flock?

To this and each of the questions that followed, the priest candidates also responded "I do."

Bishop Morrison then invited everyone in the cathedral to pray for all those who had just indicated their willingness to accept new duties of ministry in the Church. He said, "My dear people, let us pray that almighty God may pour out the gifts of heaven on these servants whom the Holy Spirit has called to be deacons and priests."

Following the Litany of the Saints, the master of ceremonies asked the deacon candidates to step forward. One by one they knelt in front of the bishop, who silently laid his hands on each of them. Then, extending his hands over them, he chanted the long prayer of consecration.

Irene glanced at her husband, wondering how he felt as he heard the words that would change their lives forever. After a while, her attention focused back on the words of the bishop: "Lord, look with favor on these servants of yours, whom we now dedicate to the office of deacon, to minister at your holy altar. Lord, send forth upon them the Holy Spirit, that they may be strengthened by the gift of your sevenfold grace to carry out faithfully the work of the ministry. May they excel in every virtue — in love that is sincere, in concern for the sick and the poor, in unassuming authority, in self-discipline, and in holiness of life. May their conduct exemplify your commandments and lead your people to imitate their purity of life. May they remain strong and steadfast in Christ, giving to the world the witness of a pure conscience. May they in this life imitate your Son, who came, not to be served but to serve, and one day reign with him in heaven."

Irene watched as Larry and the other newly ordained deacons received the symbols of their new office — the stole and dalmatic that they would wear in liturgical functions. They also accepted the Book of the Gospels, which signified their new responsibility to preach the Word of God. Finally, Bishop Morrison extended the sign of peace to each of the new deacons before they returned to their places.

Mary and T.J. watched with heightened interest as their son and the other priest candidates stepped forward for ordination. Again, the bishop laid his hands on each of their heads. But this time the concelebrating priests came forward and likewise imposed their hands on each of the candidates, signaling their own approval of the men who were about to join their ranks.

Tom's parents listened to the lengthy prayer of consecration chanted by the bishop with his arms extended over them in blessing. T.J. and Mary remembered the son who built the tree house and the tire swing in the backyard; the boy who used to chase and collect butterflies from the fields of weeds near home; the son who befriended kids who weren't always the best and the brightest and invited them to pray with him. T.J. and Mary knew he was taking the final step into a world that was much larger than theirs. As the bishop finished his prayer, they realized the ministry of priests was closely connected with the work of bishops around the globe.

"Lord, grant to these servants of yours the dignity of the priest-hood," said Bishop Morrison. "Renew within them the spirit of holiness. As coworkers with the order of bishops may they be faithful to the ministry that they receive from you, Lord God, and be to others a model of right conduct.

"May they be faithful in working with the order of bishops, so that the words of the Gospel may reach the ends of the earth, and the family of nations, made one in Christ, may become God's one, holy people."

It was at this moment that T.J. and Mary saw their son transformed into a priest before their eyes, as Tom and the other newly ordained donned chasubles such as those worn by priests at Mass. In their liturgical vestments the new priests then knelt again before the bishop while he anointed their hands with chrism, the holy oil used in many of the Church's sacramental rites. It signified the men's identification with Christ, the anointed one of God.

For a moment, T.J. thought that Bishop Morrison had forgotten about the young men kneeling in the sanctuary, because the bishop got up and walked around to the front of the altar.

"Hey, what's he doing?" he whispered to Mary.

"Shh," she said. "He's just going down to receive the offerings of bread and wine from one of the deacons, so that he can prepare them for the Mass."

"Why doesn't he at least wait until the ordination's over?"

"You'll see," replied Mary, trying to avoid getting drawn into a discussion of liturgy and theology.

Within a few minutes the answer became clear. Another deacon walked down from the altar, carrying the chalice full of wine and the paten with Communion hosts on it. He gave them to Bishop Morrison, who had resumed his seat in the presidential chair. Tom and the other new priests then knelt before the bishop, who handed them the symbols of what would be the principal ministry of their priestly lives, offering the Eucharist. As he did this, the bishop said: "Accept from the holy People of God the gifts to be offered up. Know what you are doing, and imitate the mystery you celebrate — model your life on the mystery of the Lord's Cross."

Finally, the bishop extended the sign of peace to each of the newly ordained priests, just as he had to the new deacons. He then motioned for Tom and the others, as well as the concelebrating priests, to gather with him around the altar.

As both the old and new priests began the Liturgy of the

Eucharist, Mary reached out to T.J.'s hand and held it tightly. T.J. could see the tears welling up in her eyes.

"Aw c'mon," he said, awkwardly fumbling for words of consolation. "It ain't like we've lost a son. Maybe we should think of it as having gained a Father."

Mary had to suppress a laugh as she wiped away the tears. "Oh, T.J." was all that she could manage.

More stories about faith at work in people's lives...

Sidewalks, Sacristies, and Sinners
Stories of Living Faith
by John McGowan, C.SS.R.

An inspiring collection of Gospel influenced stories and parables involving modern-day Catholics. Each story reveals Jesus is alive and working in our lives today — that we are all Gospel people with a wealth of experiences to share and much good news to pass on to others. **$2.95**

The Road Home
Five True Stories of Catholics Who Returned to the Church
by Mark Neilsen

Here are five Catholics who struggled with faith, God, and religion and left the Church. The stories of why they returned tell us much about the workings of the human heart and about the grace of God. **$2.95**

Stories of Mother Teresa
Her Smile and Her Words
By José Luis González-Balado

Stories from people of all walks of life who have known or worked with Mother Teresa share how their lives have been changed by this remarkable woman's love. This very personal work includes many of Mother Teresa's own words of faith. **$2.95**

Through a Father's Eyes
Stories of Life and Love
by Tom Sheridan

This collection of stories — tales of fatherhood, of joy, of celebration, and even of pain — contains the memories, the experiences, the life, love and faith of a father. It reminds us all of the special love that only "Dad" can give. **$1.95**

Order from your local bookstore or write to:
Liguori Publications, Box 060, Liguori, Missouri 63057-9999
*(Please add $1.00 for postage and handling for orders under $5.00;
$1.50 for orders over $5.00.)*